The All-Volunteer Army

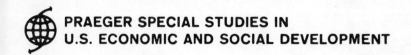

PRAEGER SPECIAL STUDIES IN
U.S. ECONOMIC AND SOCIAL DEVELOPMENT

The All-Volunteer Army

AN ANALYSIS OF DEMAND AND SUPPLY

K. H. Kim
Susan Farrell
Ewan Clague

PRAEGER PUBLISHERS
New York · Washington · London

The purpose of Praeger Special Studies is to make specialized research in U.S. and international economics and politics available to the academic, business, and government communities. For further information, write to the Special Projects Division, Praeger Publishers, Inc., 111 Fourth Avenue, New York, N.Y. 10003.

PRAEGER PUBLISHERS
111 Fourth Avenue, New York, N.Y. 10003, U.S.A.
5, Cromwell Place, London S.W.7, England

Published in the United States of America in 1971
by Praeger Publishers, Inc.

Library of Congress Catalog Card Number: 79-136142

Printed in the United States of America

FOREWORD

This study was performed by the economics department of Leo Kramer, Inc., under contract to the Directorate of Personnel Studies and Research, Office of the Deputy Chief of Staff for Personnel, Department of the Army (Contract DAHC 15 69 C 0276), and was carried out between June and September, 1969. Its purpose was to support and assist the Department of the Army in formulating its recommendations to the President's Commission on an All-Volunteer Armed Force.

The results of the study were submitted to the Army in October, 1969; this volume is a somewhat revised and edited version of that report. We are grateful to the Army for its permission to publish the results of our efforts and feel ourselves privileged to have contributed to the formation of decisions of such potential importance to the nation.

Washington, D.C.   Leo Kramer

PREFACE

The Department of Defense is the nation's largest user of manpower. For this reason alone, its need for manpower is of great interest.

This study is an outgrowth of the Army's continuing efforts to develop a comprehensive program for personnel procurement, training, distribution, retention, and separation. Its special focus is the feasibility of maintaining an all-volunteer Army.

The major concerns of the study are (1) the personnel requirements of the Army, and hence the number of young men who must be brought into the Army, in a given year and (2) the budgetary cost of paying compensation high enough to draw this required number from volunteers. The study concludes that increased compensation will attract enough volunteers to meet the armed forces' needs for personnel up to a point. Beyond that point, the cost of paying the compensation necessary to attract enough volunteers rises so sharply that an all-volunteer force becomes virtually an impossibility.

The cost of paying compensation high enough to attract enough volunteers to meet the number of men required is estimated both for the Army and for the Department of Defense as a whole. The cost estimated for the Department of Defense is based on the level of compensation necessary to attract enough volunteers to the Army. Since services other than the Army regularly draw the overwhelming preponderance of the manpower they require from volunteers, a cost estimate based on the Army's need for personnel is more valid than an estimate based on the needs of the Department of Defense as a whole. From late 1958 through the end of 1965 (the period used in this study for estimating the supply of enlistments under an all-volunteer system), there were never more than 100 inductions per fiscal year to all the other services combined.

Because of the limitations of time and resources, this study did not consider a number of important questions.

1. The draft imposes upon the nation a variety of social costs associated with inequities to and uncertainties suffered by young men of draft age. The increase in budgetary costs which this study estimates to be necessary to maintain an all-volunteer military service is offset by the elimination of some of these social costs under an all-volunteer system. For example, the increase in pay to enlisted men under an all-volunteer system will eliminate the social cost which is measured by the gap between civilian wage levels and pay received by enlisted men under the existing draft system. Other social costs which will be eliminated by establishment of an all-volunteer system were not considered in this study. Therefore, the budgetary costs estimated to be necessary to maintain an all-volunteer system may well overstate the true cost.

2. This study does not consider in full detail the budgetary savings which will flow from the higher retention rates expected to result from higher pay under an all-volunteer system. A higher retention rate leads to a savings in training costs. But since pay increases as a man advances in grade and years of service, a savings in training costs resulting from higher retention rates may be outweighed by the cost of higher pay and retirement benefits to the men retained. In order to estimate the precise amount of the net savings, it would be necessary to estimate the reenlistment rate for each job category (since job category determines training cost) and the impact of the overall retention rate on the distribution of Army personnel by years of service, pay grade, marital status, and number of dependents.

Extensive efforts were made to calculate reenlistment rates for enlisted men, but the results
were inconclusive and therefore not included in this
volume. Some experts, however, believe that turnover
will decrease by as much as 30 percent under an all-
volunteer system. If a reader cares to make this
assumption, he can derive his own crude estimate of
the savings in training costs for enlisted men under
an all-volunteer Army by taking 30 percent of the
estimated total training cost presented in Chapter 5
(in which training costs per man are established for
each Army job category for enlisted men).

3. This study does not explore the possibility
of replacing military personnel in certain job categories with civilians. The extent to which such re-
placements can be made is determined largely by the
Army's need for job spaces for the training of uniformed personnel and for rotation of uniformed personnel between United States and overseas posts.

4. This study touches only briefly on the probable racial and mental composition of the Army in the
future. Efforts were made to estimate supply equations
of enlistment and reenlistment for different racial
groups by mental categories. However, the estimated
equations were statistically insignificant. This result may be due to the fact that administratively
established enlistment standards may dictate mental
composition--and thus, indirectly, racial composition
--to a considerable degree.

5. No effort was made to consider an expanded
role for women or to analyze the role of the reserve
forces under an all-volunteer system. In the case of
the reserves, it is extremely difficult to make any
meaningful comparison with active forces because of
the complexity of the force organization of the reserves and the lack of reliable data on the "actual"
strength of reserve units.

6. In October, 1969, when the results of this
study were submitted to the Army, the President's

Commission on an All-Volunteer Armed Force had not
yet concluded its study. The Commission's report was
published in February, 1970, but its working papers
were still unavailable to the public when this study
was being prepared for publication. Since the published report of the Commission did not include a
detailed description of methodology, it was decided
not to analyze the Commission's results in this volume.

ACKNOWLEDGMENTS

This study was sponsored by the Department of the Army and carried out between June and September, 1969; it was intended to support the efforts of the Army's in-house study group on an all-volunteer Army, under the direction of Lt. Col. Jack R. Butler.

The authors gratefully acknowledge the assistance given them at every step by the staff of this study group. Particular thanks are due to Col. Butler, Lt. Col. Hector Wood, Lt. Col. David R. Hampton, and John H. Kelly. Without their help this study would have been virtually impossible.

Beyond this, the authors are indebted to the Army for the freedom afforded them throughout the study. At no time was any attempt made to circumscribe areas of investigation, to dictate approach, or to specify the tone or content of the conclusions. This openness permitted a truly inquiring and uncommitted examination of very interesting questions.

Some of the methodologies and data used in the study were originally developed in 1967-68 by K. H. Kim, one of the authors of this volume, and his former colleagues at Battelle Memorial Institute (under contract to the Army). Among those who participated in this early study, special acknowledgment is due Tom K. Lieser for his contributions to development of the inventory model and his analysis of attitudes toward military service; William K. Scheirer for his contributions to development of the inventory model; and Fred Goodman for computer programming.

For the work in this volume, thanks are due to Anthony Fisher of Brown University for his generous help in analysis of the estimated number of enlisted volunteers and, again, to Fred Goodman.

Research assistants on the project were Janice Chaplin, Michelene Hrutkay, Susan Jackson, Karen Treusch, and Susan Woods. Their patient, careful efforts in excruciatingly detailed data-gathering and manipulation are barely visible in this final product; but their work is, nevertheless, the base on which a major portion of the study is built.

The brunt of the clerical work was borne by Jane Daland; she was assisted by Patricia Griffin.

A great debt is owed to Maj. Donald S. Tribe, who was teacher and guide in the early efforts to develop a concept of military personnel procurement and who, several years ago, anticipated the need for this study. He is, in effect if not in fact, a co-author of this volume.

CONTENTS

LIST OF TABLES

xix

LIST OF FIGURES

The All-Volunteer Army

CHAPTER **1** INTRODUCTION
AND SUMMARY OF
METHODOLOGY

The central purpose of this study was to develop for the Army the first step toward a coherent, integrated approach to procurement and management of manpower under an all-volunteer system of military service.

The following areas were chosen as the primary subjects for inquiry:

1. Number of accessions (new entries into military service) needed each year in each branch/military occupational specialty/career field to maintain the Army at a specified force level for a specified period of time

2. Projected number of civilian males aged 16-26 available for military service from fiscal year 1969 to fiscal year 1980

3. Effects of certain factors exogenous to the armed forces (e.g., unemployment rates and wage levels in the civilian economy) on the supply of volunteer for military service in the past

4. Effect of competition among the services on the supply of volunteers for the Army in the past

5. Estimated number of young men who, under various circumstances, would volunteer for service as enlisted men if an all-volunteer military service were established

3

6. The cost to the Army of paying compensa-
    tion high enough to attract the number of
    volunteers needed to meet its annual re-
    quirements for accessions of enlisted men

7. The costs of compensation and training for
    all enlisted men in the Army under an all-
    volunteer system of military service

8. The cost to the Department of Defense of
    paying compensation high enough to attract
    the number of volunteers it needs to meet
    the annual requirements of all the services
    for accessions of enlisted men

9. The cost and relative effectiveness of dif-
    ferent combinations of experienced and less
    experienced enlisted men in each of the
    Army's job categories.

The procurement of officers and warrant officers
is discussed briefly, but in view of its lesser importance to an all-volunteer Army, it has not been
analyzed in such detail as the procurement of enlisted men. In addition, some effort is devoted to estimating the racial composition of an all-volunteer
Army.

Study of these subjects clearly requires both
quantitative and qualitative tools and analysis. The
major tools of quantitative analysis used in the study
were a number of computerized models developed for
the Army in the course of this study and a previous
one in 1968 by K. H. Kim et al., An Army 75 Personnel
Procurement Concept. As is always the case, lack of
data was a major problem and influenced the nature of
some of the models by limiting the refinement of their
conceptual and mathematical formulation. In general,
qualitative analysis was introduced after quantitative
measures were applied.

The methodology used in this study to identify
and analyze those factors which influence the constant flow of young men into and out of the military
services is an application of elementary concepts of

economics: demand and supply. In this case, demand
originates from the Army's force requirement and its
need to sustain a force at a specified level. Supply
is an estimate of the number of young men willing to
enlist in the Army under various circumstances.

Five groups of models were developed for the
purpose of estimating the demand for and supply of
manpower for the Army:

1. Inventory models for enlisted men, warrant
    officers, and officers

2. Civilian manpower pool model

3. Supply model for enlistments

4. Model for determining the cost and rela-
    tive effectiveness of enlisted men

5. Models for estimating compensation and
    training costs for officers and warrant
    officers.

The interrelationships of demand and supply,
and thus the interrelationships of the models, are
illustrated in Figure 1.

INVENTORY MODELS

The "demand" side of Figure 1 (the left-hand
side) consists of the inventory models. These models
simulate the changing size and composition of the
Army through time. They are a method for determining
the number of men which the Army must bring into its
ranks each year if it is to maintain a specified level
of strength. Separate models have been devised for
enlisted men, warrant officers, and officers.

The models characterize each man in the inventory by branch/military occupational specialty/career
field, pay grade, and years of service (simultaneously).
All three models can be expanded to permit description of each man in the inventory by racial group as

FIGURE 1

Methodological Overview

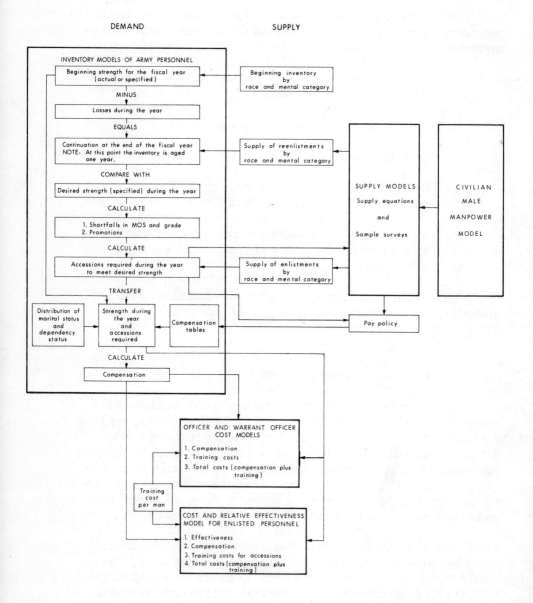

DEMAND   SUPPLY

INVENTORY MODELS OF ARMY PERSONNEL

Beginning strength for the fiscal year (actual or specified) ← Beginning inventory by race and mental category

MINUS

Losses during the year

EQUALS

Continuation at the end of the fiscal year NOTE: At this point the inventory is aged one year. ← Supply of reenlistments by race and mental category

COMPARE WITH

Desired strength (specified) during the year

CALCULATE

1. Shortfalls in MOS and grade
2. Promotions

CALCULATE

Accessions required during the year to meet desired strength ← Supply of enlistments by race and mental category

TRANSFER

Distribution of marital status and dependency status → Strength during the year and accessions required → Compensation tables

CALCULATE

Compensation

SUPPLY MODELS
Supply equations
and
Sample surveys

CIVILIAN MALE MANPOWER MODEL

Pay policy

OFFICER AND WARRANT OFFICER COST MODELS

1. Compensation
2. Training costs
3. Total costs (compensation plus training)

Training cost per man

COST AND RELATIVE EFFECTIVENESS MODEL FOR ENLISTED PERSONNEL

1. Effectiveness
2. Compensation
3. Training costs for accessions
4. Total costs (compensation plus training)

well; the model for enlisted men can be further expanded to characterize each man by mental category
(as determined by the Armed Forces Qualification
Test).

As can be seen in the diagram, the model determines not only the number of accessions needed each
year but also certain factors which enter into calculations of the costs of compensation.

SUPPLY MODELS

The right-hand side of Figure 1 depicts "supply."
Broadly speaking, supply behavior can be explained
by two basic methods: behavioral equations and attitude and socioeconomic surveys.

Behavioral equations can estimate the number of
potential volunteers who will enlist in the armed
forces in response to changes in specified variables;
the variables used in this study were the size of the
population available for military service, the level
of civilian earnings, the level of military pay, the
level of unemployment, and the level of the military's
demand for manpower.

Two equations were obtained by regression analysis: one for enlistment behavior in response to the
Army's need for accessions and one for enlistment
behavior in response to the needs of the Department
of Defense as a whole. In view of the fact that enlistments from Mental Category IV (as established by
the Armed Forces Qualification Test) have been limited in peacetime by recruitment quotas, estimates of
the supply of enlisted volunteers in this study were
limited to the supply of volunteers in Mental Categories I-III. Efforts were made to estimate supply
equations which would also explain enlistment behavior
by racial group. However, the results of these efforts were not conclusive, and they are not reported
in this volume.

Whether the number of accessions which the inventory model specifies can, in fact, be met with

volunteers is in part a function of the level of military pay. The supply equation developed during this
study provides the information necessary for determining pay policy. Specifically, the equation estimates the level of entry pay which would be sufficient
to attract the volunteers needed to meet the desired
force level. The level of military pay required is
expressed relative to the level of earnings of civilians of a comparable age group.

Of course, to understand fully the characteristics of present and future inventories of Army personnel, an estimate must be made not only of the supply
of first-term enlistments but also of the supply of
reenlistments. The estimate of reenlistment supply
made in the course of this study indicated that the
level of military pay relative to civilian pay is an
insignificant factor in the decision to reenlist.
Unfortunately, lack of detailed data makes it impossible to undertake factoral analysis of other variables
which may affect the reenlistment decision (e.g., job
security and advancement).

Detailed information on the qualitative elements
of enlistment response which cannot be measured by a
behavioral equation was obtained from attitude and
socioeconomic surveys.

CIVILIAN MANPOWER POOL MODEL

In order to calculate the potential supply of
volunteers for military service, it is necessary to
project the number of civilian males who will be available for military service. The civilian manpower
pool model was developed for this purpose.

This model estimates the number of young men in
the United States who will be aged 16-26 in each year
from fiscal 1969 to fiscal 1980, and defines them in
terms of racial group, Army recruiting district, educational attainment, marital status, and whether or
not they have children. Its crucial feature is that
it converts published data on multiple-age groups
(for example, 16- to 19-year-olds) with a single

population characteristic into descriptions of single-
year age groups (for example, 16-year-olds) by several population characteristics simultaneously.

The matrix for a single-year age group of a specified racial group in a specified Army recruiting
district in a specified year of the projection period
displays information as shown below.

	Married		Unmarried
	With depen- dents	Without depen- dents	
Enrolled: Below college In college Graduate and professional Not enrolled: High school graduate Not high school graduate			

This matrix was designed to make it easy to determine the number of men available for military service under different military manpower procurement
policies: for example, a lottery of 19-year-olds or
deferment of all undergraduate students or exemption
of all fathers. Under an all-volunteer system, the
output of the model can be used to define and locate
target populations for recruiting efforts.

The gross manpower estimates for each Army recruiting district can be reduced, if desired, by the
number of men in each age group classified by the
Selective Service System as not qualified for military
service or as qualified only in time of war or national emergency and by the number of men who were in military service or had completed military service by
the beginning of fiscal 1969.

COST AND RELATIVE EFFECTIVENESS MODEL
FOR ENLISTED PERSONNEL

The cost and relative effectiveness model calculates three alternative mixes of first-termers and careerists for a force of a given size. (First-termers are enlisted personnel with less than three years of service; careerists are enlisted personnel with three or more years of service.) These mixes are the following:

1. The mix actually specified by the inventory model for enlisted men, whether the force simulated in the inventory is actual or hypothetical

2. The wage-optimum mix for a force of that size (the mix at which the Army maximizes the effectiveness of its enlisted force, given budget constraints and a specified ratio of the wages of first-termers to those of careerists; or the mix at which the Army minimizes budgetary costs, given a specified wage ratio and level of effectiveness)

3. The MOS (military occupational specialty)-optimum mix (the technologically desired mix) for a force of that size (the mix which, regardless of cost, best utilizes the skills and experience levels of first-termers and careerists for a force of the given size).

These mixes are calculated for each job category (MOS) and for enlisted men in the Army as a whole. The model then calculates an index of effectiveness for each mix and the wage and training costs associated with that mix for a force of the size specified. Next, it calculates the ratio of cost to effectiveness for each mix and the ratios of the index of effectiveness of one mix to the index of effectiveness of another mix. All these calculations are performed for each MOS and for enlisted strength as a whole.

The model also calculates trade-offs between
first-termers and careerists, i.e., the number of
first-termers needed to replace one careerist in order
to keep effectiveness at the same level; these trade-
offs are calculated for each MOS and for the Army as
a whole. Also calculated are the maximum career pre-
miums--i.e., the maximum amount it would pay the Army
to offer a careerist to induce him to remain in the
Army if he intends to leave; these, too, are calculated for each MOS and for the Army as a whole. However, maximum career premiums are calculated only for
the mix of first-termers and careerists actually specified by the inventory model. Maximum career premiums are zero in a wage-optimum or MOS-optimum mix.

The model can be used to calculate differential
wages for those MOSs which reflect shortages of experienced men. The shortage of experienced men in
an MOS is a factor in the Army's definition of the
"criticality" of an MOS. Estimates are also made of
the cost of wages and the cost of wages plus training
under each mix.

All of the calculations listed above are later
adjusted to reflect differences in the proficiency
ratings of first-termers in different years-of-service
categories within an MOS.

This model is designed to permit exploration of
the effects of different wage policies and mixes of
experience levels (in each MOS and in the Army as a
whole) for a force of a given size and determination
of the demand of the force for first-termers. For
example, if the Army's personnel policy with respect
to career mix is wage-optimal, the desired net change
in the proportion of first-termers (or, equivalently,
the desired number of accessions) can be determined
by the model, given the loss rates of first-termers
and careerists. This change in the proportion of
first-termers is directly relevant to calculation of
the level of entry pay sufficient to induce enough
volunteers to maintain a volunteer army. Furthermore,
the rate of personnel turnover could be lowered by
payment of the maximum career premium suggested by
this model.

OFFICER COST MODELS

Officer cost models estimate compensation and/or training costs for the inventories of officers and warrant officers specified by the inventory models. Costs are estimated for each branch and for officers or warrant officers as a whole.

INTERRELATIONSHIPS OF THE MODELS

As Figure 1 illustrates, the interrelationships of the inventory model for enlisted men, the supply models, and the civilian manpower pool model are very close. Some of these interrelationships are immediately apparent. For example, the accessions specified as necessary by the inventory model must be drawn from available manpower, and any characteristic of the young male population available for military service (as determined by the civilian manpower pool model) is reflected in present and future inventories of Army personnel.

Figure 1 also makes explicit several relationships between the supply models and the inventory model for enlisted men. Note, for example, the arrows which flow from "supply of reenlistments" to "continuation at the end of fiscal year" and from "supply of enlistments" to "accessions required." It is clear, too, that a great deal of information calculated by the inventory model is used as data in the model for determining the cost and relative effectiveness of enlisted personnel.

Other interrelationships of the models are a function of the nature of an all-volunteer military service--in which all accessions are, by definition, enlistments. As explained above, the inventory model for enlisted men determines the number of accessions of enlisted men needed each year to maintain a force of a given size. The size of the population available for military service (as determined by the civilian manpower pool model) clearly determines the enlistment rate necessary to obtain the accessions required. This enlistment rate, in turn, affects the ratio of military pay to civilian pay necessary to attract the number of volunteers needed. The pay ratio is the output of the supply equation and ultimately affects the cost of compensating the entire inventory of enlisted men.

Still other interrelationships of the models are not at all apparent in Figure 1. For example, the number of young men estimated to be available for military service by the civilian manpower pool model is used, for projection purposes, as a variable in the supply equation.

CONCLUSION

It is evident that the size and structure of the force desired, the size of the population available for military service, the rate of reenlistment, the number of enlisted accessions required, military pay policy, and the relative effectiveness of enlisted personnel jointly determine the feasibility of maintaining an all-volunteer Army. Since each of these variables is continually changing through time, the nature of the interactions between the models developed in this study is not only close but also dynamic.

CHAPTER **2** THE
INVENTORY
MODELS

As was explained in Chapter 1, the inventory
models simulate the changing size and composition of
the Army through time. They were designed to project
the number of accessions required by the Army in each
enlisted career field, officer branch, and warrant
officer branch or MOS* under varying force levels and
force structures.

Required accessions are generated separately for
enlisted men, warrant officers, and officers for each
fiscal year over a specified number of years under
different scenarios. (A scenario is defined as required Army strength for the period of the simulation;
the level of strength required may be either actual
or hypothetical.)

Data and methodology used in the inventory models
are described below. While the projection of accession requirements is the raison d'être of the models,
a large amount of other useful information is generated as intermediate output and is also described below.
As will be seen, the availability and suitability of
data often imposed significant limitations on the level of detail used in the models.

---

*Army job categories are described by numbers
ranging from one to five digits; the greater the number of digits, the greater the degree of detail in
which the job is described. A two-digit job category
is a career field. A three-digit job category is a
military occupational specialty, commonly referred
to as an MOS.

One computer run of the models was made for this study. The force structure specified in the run was a hypothetical force of a size deemed adequate for "peacekeeping." It was provided by the Department of the Army. Since some of the output of the inventory models is classified information, the detailed results of this run cannot be reproduced in this book.

Simulation begins with the reading of a scenario --that is, with the reading of required Army strength for the period of the simulation. After reading a scenario, the model computes the desired number of officers, warrant officers, or enlisted men in the inventory (whichever group is being simulated by the model). In making this computation, the model uses the desired proportions of enlisted men, officers, and warrant officers for the total Army strength required. This relationship has been read into a preliminary program, which has put it on magnetic tape to be used by the inventory model whenever needed. The same is true of other relationships used later in the model. The desired number is computed for each year of the simulation period, beginning with the first year of the scenario. If the year being simulated is the first year of the scenario, the computer reads in the beginning inventory of personnel from the tape produced by the preliminary program. This inventory is classified by grade, year of service, and branch/MOS/career field simultaneously.

The computer next reads data on marital and dependency status by grade and years of service, and then generates the information necessary for calculating average pay and allowances for men in their first three years of service and for men with more years of service. This information is generated for each branch/MOS/career field. The computer also calculates many statistics which summarize the inventory in various ways.

Next the computer considers continuation, which is defined as the continuance of a man in the inventory for another year. It first selects or computes continuation rates, selection or computation depending upon the scenario and preferences expressed by

the user. These continuation rates are the percentages of men who can be expected to continue in service during the year under consideration. Like the
inventory, they are classified by grade, year of service, and branch/MOS/career field. The computer then
applies these continuation rates to the inventory to
obtain the number of personnel continuing.

The computer then calculates desired strength
in each branch/MOS/career field, using a functional
relationship for this purpose. It then compares this
desired strength with the number of personnel continuing in that branch/MOS/career field to obtain
the number of accessions required or the size of the
personnel surplus in each branch/MOS/career field.

The year of service of all personnel continuing
is then increased by one. The accessions required,
if any, in each branch/MOS/career field are then added into the inventory of personnel continuing for
that branch/MOS/career field. Officer and enlisted
accessions are assumed to be in their first year of
service; warrant officer accessions are assumed to be
in their second year of service. It is assumed that
all accessions are in the lowest grade. It is im-
plicitly assumed that the accessions required are actually procured.

The computer then calculates the desired strength
in each grade in each branch/MOS/career field, using
a set of functional relationships for this purpose.
Personnel are then "promoted" one grade to attain the
desired strengths in each grade. Selection for promotion is based on year of service (personnel with
more years of service being selected for promotion
first). If necessary, the computer dips down another
grade to obtain the desired number of personnel. The
computer also calculates overall promotion rates by
grade and year of service.

If the computer has been simulating events during the last year of a scenario, it reads another
scenario (if there is one) and proceeds as before.
If the last year of the scenario has not yet been
reached, the computer goes to the next year of

scenario, calculates the desired number of officers,
warrant officers, or enlisted men and proceeds as
before.

THE PROCESS IN DETAIL

For each scenario, the computer simulates the
inventory, continuation, promotion, and accessions
during each year of the scenario. Each simulation
covers a specified number of years. A given year of
the simulation is designated by t. If each scenario
is simulated for the full number of years and if simulation begins with fiscal 1969, then t=1 represents
fiscal 1969 and t=12 represents fiscal 1980, which
is T, the last year of simulation.

Definitions of Data

N_t is total active Army strength, net of fed-
eralized reserves, needed by the end of period t, including enlisted women and female officers and warrant officers. N_t is read into the computer for each
year from t=1 to t=T. This set of numbers is the
scenario.

P_t is the proportion of Army strength (N_t) needed as enlisted men, warrant officers, or officers by
the end of period t. For officers, this proportion
historically has been very volatile, and it is therefore calculated by the computer, using a set of equations in the form $P_t = \alpha + \beta N_t$. As N_t attains a
specified level, the appropriate α and β are called
up to calculate the proportion of officers. This
proportion ranges from a maximum of .115 when N_t =
1,000,000 or less (a "peacekeeping" level) to a minimum of .075 when N_t = 3,000,000 or more (a "major
war" level), reflecting the lead time necessary to
procure officers during a buildup in Army strength.
For this study, a constant proportion specified by
the Army was used for each year t. In the equations,
β is the rate of change in P_t (the proportion of officers) associated with the change in the size of the
Army; α is the portion of P_t which does not change
with the size of the Army.

The proportion of warrant officers can be specified to vary in the same manner as the proportion
of officers. For this study, however, a constant
proportion was used for each year, as specified by
the Army.

For enlisted men, P_t is the residual--i.e., P_t
for enlisted men = 1-(P_t for warrant officers) -(P_t
for officers), so that the three proportions sum to
one. Since P_t for both warrant officers and officers
was specified at a constant level for each year in
the run of the model made for this study, P_t for enlisted men is also constant for each year.

n_t is the number of men needed as enlisted men,
warrant officers, or officers for the Army strength
desired by the end of period t, which is simply equal
to $P_t(N_t)$. For an Army strength (N_t) of 1,000,000,
for example, n_t for officers = .115 (1,000,000) =
115,000 officers if P_t for officers is .115.

Definitions of Variables

$i_{g,y,t}^k$ is the number of men (enlisted men, warrant officers, or officers) in the kth branch/MOS/
career field, the gth grade, and the yth year of service at the beginning of period t. The feasible level
of detail, the lesser relevance of primary MOS in officer assignment and promotion, and the availability
of suitable data all argued for the treatment of officers by branch rather than by MOS. It should be
noted that y measures active federal service for enlisted men and warrant officers, but active federal
commissioned service for officers. When y = 31, the
individuals are in their 31st year of service or more.
The k denotes the branch/MOS/career field in the beginning inventory. Thereafter, it is assumed that
each person's branch/MOS/career field remains the
same.* The beginning inventory, representing actual

---

*This is, of course, a serious limitation. How-
ever, only about 5 per cent of officers have a branch
designation different from their branch at the time of

or specified active Army strength for the beginning
of the most recent fiscal year (t=1), is read into
the computer. The computer calculates the inventory
for later years from t=2 to t=T+1. The inventories
contain the levels of detail shown below.

	Enlisted Men	Warrant Officers	Officers
k	62	12	22*
g	9	4	5**
y	31	31	31

The computer program limits on k, g, and y are thus
62, 9, and 31, respectively. To go beyond these limits would require reprogramming. However, the program
as it exists can accommodate warrant officers by MOS,
up to the limit of 62. The 62 enlisted career fields
(listed in Table 18) are the same as those found in

commissioning--much less a designation different from
their branch during the 10 years under consideration.
Transfers of enlisted men from one career field to
another are about 2-3 percent per year of all enlisted men. If a scenario covers 10 years, then 20-30
percent of the enlisted men in the inventory of the
last year of simulation will have incorrect career
fields. The data that do exist on such transfers are
not available by grade or year of service, making
them difficult to incorporate into the model.

     *The first 15 branches are Army Promotion List
(APL) branches; the last seven are non-APL specialist
branches. Professors at the U.S. Military Academy
(USMA) are combined with infantry because a USMA pro-
fessor is at least a lieutenant colonel and the model
allows for additions to a branch only by accessions
at the level of lieutenant. The effect is, of course,
small.

     **General officers excluded; first and second
lieutenants combined.

AR 611-201 (C5), "Enlisted Military Occupational Spe-
cialties," dated February 12, 1968.* For officers
and warrant officers, each branch was denoted by a
number according to the sequence below.

<u>Officer Branches</u>   <u>Warrant Officer Branches</u>

 1. Infantry   1. Artillery
 2. Field Artillery   2. Aviation
 3. Air Defense   3. Ordnance
 4. Armor   4. Quartermaster
 5. Chemical Corps   5. Military Intelligence
 6. Corps of Engineers   6. Engineer
 7. Ordnance Corps   7. Signal Corps
 8. Quartermaster   8. Transportation
 9. Signal Corps   9. Adjutant General
10. Transportation Corps   10. Military Police
11. Adjutant General   11. Judge Advocate General
12. Finance Corps   12. Medical Service Corps
13. Military Police
14. Military Intelligence
15. Women's Army Corps
16. Chaplain
17. Judge Advocate General
18. Medical Corps
19. Dental Corps
20. Veterinarians Corps
21. Medical Service Corps
22. Army Nurse Corps

For all years from t=1 through t=T+1, the $i_{g,y,t}^{k}$
cells are aggregated in several different ways in

---

*References to Department of Defense (DOD) and
Army documents which appear in this and other chap-
ters of this study are often incomplete. In some
cases, this is so because DOD or the Army did not
print on a document all the information necessary for
a technically correct reference. In other cases, references were deliberately abbreviated by the authors;
this was done whenever a document is more familiarly
known within the Army by an abbreviated title (or
number), and thus more easily located by a researcher
if it is requested by that title.

the printout in order to facilitate analysis. Separate calculations are made for enlisted men, warrant
officers, and officers.

$i^k_{y,t}$ is the inventory by branch/MOS/career field
and year of service (aggregated over all grades).

$i^k_{g,t}$ is the inventory by branch/MOS/career field
and grade (aggregated over all years of service).

$i_{g,y,t}$ is the inventory by grade and year of
service (aggregated over all branches/MOSs/career
fields).

i^k_t is the inventory by branch/MOS/career field
(aggregated over all grades and years of service).

$i_{q,t}$ is the inventory by grade (aggregated over
all branches/MOSs/career fields and years of service).

$i_{y,t}$ is the inventory by year of service (aggregated over all grades and branches/MOSs/career fields).

i_t is the total inventory at the beginning of
year t.

Certain cells are then combined to calculate
branch/MOS/career field proportions and first-termer/
careerist mixes for each branch/MOS/career field for
each year t=1 through t=T+1, as follows:

The proportion of each branch/MOS/career field
to the total inventory is obtain by dividing i^k_t by i_t.

The ratio of first-termers to careerists* is
obtained by dividing the inventory for each branch/
MOS/career field with less than three years of service by the inventory for the same branch/MOS/career
field of those with three or more years of service.

---

*In this and all subsequent first-termer/careerist
calculations, a first-termer is a person with fewer
than three years of service, and a careerist is a person with three or more years of service.

The proportion of first-termers who are in their first year is determined by dividing the inventory of first-year first-termers for each branch/MOS/career field by the inventory of all first-termers for the same branch/MOS/career field.

The proportion of first-termers who are in their second year is found by dividing the inventory of second-year first-termers for each branch/MOS/career field by the inventory of all first-termers for the same branch/MOS/career field.

The continuation rate, denoted as $r_{g,y,t}^k$, is the proportion of men in the beginning inventory for a given $i_{g,y,t}^k$ cell which is still in the inventory at the end of the year--that is, the proportion of men not lost during the year. This rate is equal to one minus the loss rate.

When Army strength desired by the end of period t equals or exceeds 2,000,000 men, it is assumed that partial or total federalization of reserves has begun and men are "frozen in" for the duration of the conflict. In this case, the computer reads in a set of special loss rates, denoted as $\bar{\bar{s}}$, which reflect the attrition due to battle casualties, nonbattle deaths and disabilities, and other losses incidental to the combat situation. The $\bar{\bar{s}}$'s are defined as follows:

$\bar{\bar{s}}_g^k$ is the loss rate in the kth career field/branch by grade for $N_t \geq 2,000,000$.

$\bar{\bar{s}}$ is the overall loss rate for officers, warrant officers, or enlisted men for $N_t \geq 2,000,000$.

Both $\bar{\bar{s}}_g^k$ and $\bar{\bar{s}}$ were derived from the Army's experience during World War II. However, when a certain $\bar{\bar{s}}_g^k$ seemed unusual, judgmental adjustments (on the basis of $\bar{\bar{s}}$) were made. In order to determine $\bar{\bar{s}}_{g,y}^k$ (loss rate in the kth career field/branch by grade and years of service), the assumption is made that for all t

$$\bar{\bar{s}}_{g,y,t}^k = \bar{\bar{s}}_{g,y}^k = \bar{\bar{s}}_g^k$$

With the specified $\bar{\bar{s}}^k_{g,y,t}$, the computer then
calculates the continuation rate during a period of
mobilization. This rate is denoted as $\bar{\bar{r}}$, and is defined as

$$\bar{\bar{r}}^k_{g,y,t} = 1-.01 - \bar{\bar{s}}^k_{g,y,t}$$

In the right-hand side of the above equation, the 1
reflects the "freeze-in" assumption, the .01 is a
deduction for administrative losses, and the $\bar{\bar{s}}$ term
is as defined above. It should be noted that $\bar{\bar{r}}$ varies
in effect only by career field/branch and grade, because of a lack of casualty data by year of service.

When desired strength for the end of period t is
less than 2,000,000 men, the continuation rates are
calculated on the basis of historically observed loss
rates during a nonmobilization period. The loss rates
used for this study are discussed later in this chapter.

The number of men continuing during each year t
of a given scenario is calculated by multiplying the
inventory cell for a given k, g, and y at the beginning of that year by the continuation rate during that
year for the same k, g, and y. These continuation
numbers then replace the corresponding inventory cells
in computer memory. The same ratios and proportions
which were calculated for the inventory, as described
above, are then calculated for the continuation. The
continuation cells are denoted as $R^k_{g,y,t}$.

Determination of Accessions Needed by Branch/MOS/Career Field

At this point, the computer memory contains the
total number of personnel continuing during year t,
the desired end strength (N_t) for year t, and the number (n_t) who are enlisted men, warrant officers, or
officers, as the case may be. The computer now calculates the proportions ($p_{k,t}$) of n_t desired in each
of the k branches/MOSs/career fields by the end of
year t.

The user has the option of varying the proportions of men in each branch/MOS/career field according to n_t, to allow for increasing proportions (relative growth) in some and decreasing proportions (relative decline) in others. The computer contains the function

$$p_{k,t} = \alpha_k + \beta_k n_t$$

for each k. The α_k's and β_k's, having no time subscript, are constant. If $\beta_k = 0$ for each k, the proportion of men in each branch/MOS/career field will be constant regardless of n_t. On the other hand, if β_k is positive for a given branch/MOS/career field, $p_{k,t}$ will be larger than α_k--and vice versa if β_k is negative. Since the p_k's are proportions, their sum over all k must equal 1. The same is true for the α_k's. The β_k's must sum to zero, however, since growing proportions in some branches/MOSs/career fields must be offset by decreasing proportions in others to assure that the sum of p_k's will be 1. In the computer run made for this study, the β_k's were set at zero for each k, thus assuming constant branch/MOS/career field proportionality regardless of n_t. With the p_k's now in the computer, the number of men desired in each branch/MOS/career field (n_k) is calculated by multiplying p_k by n_t.

The computer is now ready to calculate accessions (a_k) for each MOS/branch. As with any business-oriented annual inventory model, the replacement requirements (accessions) represent the "new purchases" required to fill the depletion of stock, or "sales" (losses) during the year, plus any growth in the planned stock (desired strength) for the beginning of the next year. Continuation simply represents the end-of-year stock, or initial stock less sales. Thus, for each MOS/branch,

Accessions = Desired Strength - Continuation.

When the desired proportion of an MOS in the inventory decreases, or when overall desired strength is decreasing, or both, it is possible that the computer will calculate negative accessions for some MOSs (i.e., if continuation is greater than desired strength, accessions will be negative). In such a case, the computer prints a message that accessions for these MOSs/branches are negative, but does not subtract or otherwise dispose of them. Instead, negative accessions are considered a "surplus" (s_k) in the continuation and are left in the inventory for the beginning of the next year. It is therefore true that the inventory (i_{t+1}^k) for a given branch/MOS/career field at the beginning of the following year will exceed the desired strength (n_t^k) by the amount of the surplus (s_k). Surpluses are maintained in the inventory because their removal (which means forcing men out of a branch/MOS/career field or out of the Army altogether) would have to be based on criteria involving much more data (perhaps an individual file for each man in the Army) than could possibly be handled by this model.

When the accessions (a_k) for a given MOS/branch are negative, the computer redefines a_k as zero (although the surpluses, as discussed above, remain in the inventory). The redefined a_k's, which are now greater than or equal to zero for all branches, are summed to obtain the total number of accessions needed during period t.

"Aging" of the Continuation

The continuation numbers ($R_{g,y,t}^k$ cells) in the computer memory are now "aged" by redefining the number in each continuation cell as being in the next year-of-service cell. For example, the R_g^k who were in their first year of service (y=1) in the continuation are now found in the second year-of-service cell for the new inventory; second-year men now become third-year men, and so forth. The final year-of-service cell (y=31+) is not redefined, since this is the upper limit of the y subscript; instead, the previous year's 30-year men are added to the men who continue in the 31+ year cell.

Adding in the Accessions

After the continuation cells have been aged, the cells for all k and g for the first year of service

will be empty. The accessions are now added into
these cells and thus become the first-year men in the
new inventory.

An exception to the above procedure is made for
warrant officers. The inventory of warrant officers,
consisting of actual strength taken from the COPO-11
Report for June 30, 1967, showed only 77 warrant officers in their first year of service but 2,110 in
their second year of service. Discussion of this
data with knowledgeable Department of the Army offi-
cials revealed that, on the average, warrant officers
spend about one year as enlisted men before they are
commissioned as warrant officers. Consequently, it
was decided to add the warrant officer accessions for
each year into the second year-of-service cell $(i_{g,2}^k)$
rather than the first-year cell $(i_{g,1}^k)$. Since this
year's warrant officer accessions were enlisted men
in last year's inventory, this procedure must be fol-
lowed in order to avoid double-counting of the warrant officers during a given year.

Since the inventory model is run separately for
enlisted men, officers, and warrant officers, there
is no transfer of data from one category (e.g., warrant officers) to another (e.g., enlisted men).
Where possible, however, modifications such as the
above are made in order to keep the simulation as
realistic as possible.

Desired Number of Men in Each Grade

Officers

The proportion of officers desired in each grade
for each year t of a given scenario is denoted as d_g.
The d_g are expressed as proportions of desired
strength plus surpluses.

The d_g can be specified by a planning document
or can be based on the Officer Grade Limitation Act
(OGLA) of 1954 (Section 3202, Title 10, United States
Code). In the run of the model made for this report,
they are specified by a planning document on the hypothetical force being simulated. Ordinarily, however,

the data used for calculating the d_g for field grade officers are the strengths by grade authorized by the OGLA; the strength authorized in each grade varies with the total number of officers authorized. The OGLA data are summarized in Table 1. Regression analyses were performed on the d_g, using the "total number authorized" as the independent variable (n_t+s_t) and the proportion of authorized strength in a given grade (d_g) as the dependent variable. A separate regression was performed for each of the three field grades. It was found that a semilogarithmic equation of the form

$$\ln d_g = \alpha_g + \beta_g (n_t+s_t)$$

provided the best estimates (call them $\hat{\alpha}_g$ and $\hat{\beta}_g$) of α_g and β_g. The estimated equations for field-grade officers are as follows:

Grade 1: Colonels

$$\ln d_1 = -2.4612-.000005213 \ (n_t+s_t) \quad \overline{R}^2=.9931$$
$$(.0000001)$$

Grade 2: Lieutenant Colonels

$$\ln d_2 = 1.8750-.0000021503 \ (n_t+s_t) \quad \overline{R}^2=.9932$$
$$(.0000001)$$

Grade 3: Majors

$$\ln d_3 = -1.5824-.0000018544 \ (n_t+s_t) \quad \overline{R}^2=.9985$$
$$(.0000001)$$

Grade 4: Captains

Since the OGLA does not apply to company-grade officers, a separate regression was performed for captains, using the same equation as above. The data used in this case were a time-series on total actual officer strength (n_t+s_t), abstracted from the DCSPER-46 Report, and a time-series on the actual proportions of (n_t+s_t) that were captains, abstracted from the same report. The following estimate was obtained for captains:

TABLE 1

Officer Grade Limitation Act of 1954, Army Section

Authorized Strength in Specified Grades

Total Number of Officers Authorized[a]	Colonels		Lt. Colonels		Majors	
	n[b]	p[c]	n	p	n	p
49,650	3,352	.067	6,940	.139	9,350	.187
59,600	3,752	.063	8,045	.134	10,950	.183
69,575	4,102	.059	9,150	.131	12,500	.179
79,550	4,452	.056	10,205	.128	14,050	.176
89,525	4,752	.053	11,260	.125	15,600	.173
99,505	5,002	.050	12,265	.123	17,060	.171
109,490	5,202	.047	13,270	.121	18,370	.167
119,480	5,402	.045	14,175	.118	19,680	.164
129,470	5,602	.043	15,075	.116	20,890	.161
139,460	5,802	.041	15,875	.113	22,095	.158
149,450	6,002	.040	16,675	.111	23,300	.155

[a] Excluding general officers.
[b] Number authorized in grade.
[c] Proportion of total number of officers authorized.

Source: Officer Grade Limitation Act of 1954, U.S. Code, Title 10, Sec. 3202.

$$\ln d_4 = -.56429-.000006276 \ (n_t+s_t) \quad \overline{R}^2=.9507$$
$$(.0000001)$$

It is important to note at this point, lest the reader be misled by the high values of the coefficients of determination ($\overline{R}^2$ greater than .95 in every case), that these four equations yield reliable estimates of d_g only within the range of the (n_t+s_t) data used in estimating them (total officer strength from 50,000 to 150,000). The estimated d_g's steadily decline as total strength increases, reflecting the data on which they are based. These equations can, however, lead to unrealistically low estimates of d_g if total officer strength is high enough. For example, if total officer strength (n_t+s_t) is 500,000, the estimated d_g for colonels would be

$$\ln d_1 = -2.4612-.000005213 \ (500,000)$$

$$= -2.4612-2.6065$$

$$= -5.0677$$

$$d_1 = \quad .0063, \text{ or } .63 \text{ percent}$$

It was therefore necessary to impose "floors" on each of the estimated d_g's. If the estimated value is less than the floor value for a given grade, the computer uses the floor value in calculating the desired number of officers for that grade. The floor values used were the stabilized values reached during World War II (see the DCSPER-46 Report) as follows:

Grade	Floor on d_g
Colonel	.013
Lieutenant Colonel	.035
Major	.084
Captain	.207

Grade 5: Lieutenants

The desired proportion of lieutenants (d_5) is simply expressed as a residual of the sum of d_g's calculated for the grades above (1,2,3, and 4).

Since the d_g's sum to one,

$$d_5 = 1-(d_1+d_2+d_3+d_4)$$

This is true regardless of whether estimated values or floor values are used for d_1 through d_4.

With the values of d_g, whether specified or estimated, now in computer memory, the next step is to specify the desired proportion of men in each branch for each grade ($d_{g,k}$). The $d_{g,k}$ are either specified by a planning document or based on past experience. In this report, the $d_{g,k}$ are specified by a planning document.

The computer then calculates the desired number of officers in the gth grade for the kth branch, denoted as $n_{g,k}$:

$$n_{g,k} = d_{g,k}(n_k+s_k)$$

Enlisted Men and Warrant Officers

The proportion of men desired in each career field/MOS/branch and grade ($d_{g,k}$) and the number desired in each career field/MOS/branch and grade ($n_{g,k}$) are defined as they were for officers. The $d_{g,k}$ are calculated by the computer from the equation

$$\ln d_{g,k} = \alpha_{g,k} + \beta_{g,k}(n_k+s_k)$$

in which the $\beta_{g,k}$ may be used to vary the proportion of men in a given career field/MOS/branch and grade to express a relative growth or decline in that $n_{g,k}$ cell. In the run of the model made for this study, the $\beta_{g,k}$ were read in as zeros, assuming a constant mix by career field/MOS/branch and grade. The $n_{g,k}$ were calculated as they were for officers.

Promotion.

Career Field/MOS/Branch-Dependent Promotion

The following career field/MOS/branch-specific promotion procedure applies to enlisted men, warrant officers, and the last seven officer branches (the non-APL specialist branches). The procedure begins with the highest grade (g=1).

First, $s_{g,k}$ is defined as the shortfall in the gth grade for the kth career field/MOS/branch (to be distinguished from the previous use of s_k to represent the surplus for a given k). For a given (g,k) cell,

Shortfall = Desired Strength - Continuation.

If the shortfall is zero, no promotion into the gth grade from men one grade lower (grade g+1) is necessary. The computer then computes the shortfall $(s_{g+1,k})$, if any, for one grade lower and proceeds as before.

If the shortfall is less than zero, there are too many men in the gth grade. The computer then reduces the desired number of men one grade lower by the amount of the negative shortfall. For example, if there are 50 men in grade E-9 continuing in a given career field, but desired strength for grade E-9 in this MOS is only 40 men, the shortfall is equal to 40-50, or -10. The computer then adds the negative shortfall for E-9s to the strength of E-8s in the same career field. If there are initially 100 men in grade E-8, the computer redefines desired E-8 strength as 100 + (-10), or 90. It then considers promotion to grade E-8 by calculating the shortfall, if any, for grade E-8 in this career field. The shortfall will be equal to the new strength of 90 minus the continuation of E-8s for this career field. The computer then proceeds as before.

If the shortfall for a given career field/MOS/ branch and grade is greater than zero, there are too few men in that grade, and it is necessary to promote to that grade a number of men equal to the shortfall. The men to be promoted are selected first by grade, then by year of service (men having the most years of service being promoted first). If the number of men in a given grade and year of service is larger than the number needed for promotion at that point, the

computer promotes only the number needed. If, on
the other hand, the number of men in a given grade
and year of service is less than the number needed
for promotion, all men in that year of service are
promoted and the computer proceeds to successively
lower years of service until promotion needs are completely filled. If a positive shortfall still exists
when the computer has promoted the men in all years
of service for a given grade, it moves down another
grade and continues the same procedure until promotion needs are met.

For example, if the number of men continuing in
a given career field and grade E-9 is 50, but desired
strength is 100, 50 men must be promoted to grade
E-9. The computer first promotes E-8s with 31+ years
of service; then, if a shortfall still exists, E-8s
with 30 years of service; and so on until needs are
met. If the shortfall still exists after all E-8s
with less than one year of service have been promoted
(i.e., there are fewer than 50 men in grade E-8), the
computer moves down to E-7s with 31+ years of service
and continues the same procedures until E-9 strength
reaches 100 men. It must then go through the same
process for grade E-8, which may have been emptied
by E-9 promotion requirements.

When the lowest grade is reached, the shortfall
is equal to zero, since desired strength will have
been met by accessions.

Nonbranch-Dependent Promotion for APL Branches

For the first 15 officer branches (the APL
branches) it is assumed that men in one branch can
be promoted on the basis of the needs of another
branch. The number of officers desired in a given
grade is therefore the number desired for that grade
in all 15 branches combined, rather than for one
branch at a time. However, when officers are promoted, and thus shifted from one matrix cell to another in the computer, their branch classification
remains the same.

Since the classification of officers by branch
is preserved, but branch is ignored as a criterion

for selecting officers for promotion, a special problem arises. If the number of officers in a given
grade and year of service cell is greater than the
number needed from that cell for promotion to the
next grade, the problem is how many officers to promote from each branch. In this case, an equal percentage of officers (in that grade and year of service) is promoted from each branch.

Promotion Statistics

The computer prints the proportion of men promoted by their original grade and year of service,
aggregated over all branches/MOSs/career fields. It
also prints the number of men desired in each grade
in each branch/MOS/career field and the number of men
promoted from each grade of each branch/MOS/career
field into the next grade (zero, of course, for the
top grade in every case). The number of men promoted
from each grade is not given for each APL officer
branch; it is given only for the 15 APL branches taken
together, since promotion is not branch-dependent in
these branches.

Final Inventory

The computer, having completed a full simulation
cycle, now contains the entire inventory for the beginning of year t+1. It proceeds by performing a full
simulation cycle for each succeeding year through year
T, ending with the beginning inventory for year T+1.

Flexibility of the Model

It should be emphasized that the inventory model
is extremely flexible. Any input can be altered in
any way to suit either the real world or the needs of
the analyst. Among the inputs that can be altered
are the following:

1. The active Army strength desired (the
    scenario)

2. The number of years of simulation

3. The first year of the simulation

4. The inventory which begins the simulation
    (it can be actual or hypothetical)

5. The proportion of men desired as officers,
    warrant officers, and enlisted men

6. The continuation rates

7. The proportion of men desired in each
    branch/MOS/career field

8. The proportion of men desired in each grade

9. The floor on the proportion of men desired
    in each grade.

The last five inputs are examples of managed or
policy variables, which can be altered to reflect
policies assumed for the simulation. For example,
the continuation rates could be altered to explore
the effects of a mandatory retirement policy during
a phasedown scenario.

ESTIMATES OF PAY

The large amount of information contained in the
inventory model permits calculation of the average
pay of first-termers and careerists in each MOS or
branch, based on grade and years of service. Pay is
defined as the tax-equivalent total of basic pay,
quarters and subsistence allowances, and medical, retirement, and other fringe benefits.[1]

Calculation of Marital Status and Dependents

The first step in calculation of pay is calculation of the distribution of marital status and number
of dependents, on which pay partly depends.

Enlisted Men and Officers

After it has calculated the inventory by k, g,
and y, the computer reads in two sets of data for each
year t of a given scenario:

$(MS)_{g,m}$ = marital status by grade.
$(DP)_{g,d}$ = dependency status by grade.

$(MS)_{g,m}$ has two values for each grade:

If m = 1, $(MS)_g$ = proportion of single men
in gth grade.

m = 2, $(MS)_g$ = proportion of married men
in gth grade.

$(DP)_{g,d}$ has six values for each grade:

If d = 0, $(DP)_g$ = proportion of single men
in gth grade.

d = 1, $(DP)_g$ = proportion of married men
without children in gth
grade.

d = 2, $(DP)_g$ = proportion of married men
with one child in gth grade.

d = 3, $(DP)_g$ = proportion of married men
with two children in gth
grade.

d = 4, $(DP)_g$ = proportion of married men
with three children in gth
grade.

d = 5, $(DP)_g$ = proportion of married men
with four or more children
in gth grade.

The computer then calculates

$$i_g^k \times (MS)_{g,m} = (iMS)_{g,m}^k \quad \text{for m = 1 and 2}$$

Thus the inventory for the kth MOS/branch and the gth
grade is multiplied by the proportion of single (or
married) men in that grade to obtain the number of
single (or married) men in that grade and MOS/branch.

If m = 1 (single), the computer calculates

$$(iMS)^k_{g,1} \; \times \; \frac{i^k_{g,y}}{i^k_g} \; = \; (iMS)^k_{g,y,o}$$

That is, each inventory cell of single men by grade
and branch/MOS/career field is distributed over the
years-of-service categories by multiplying it by the
ratio of inventory by k, g, and y to the inventory
by k and g.

If m = 2 (married), the computer calculates for
d = 1 to 5:

$$(iMS)^k_{g,2} \; \times \; (DP)_{g,d} \; = \; (iMSDP)^k_{g,d}$$

That is, the number of married men in a given branch/
MOS/career field and grade is multiplied by the proportion of men in that grade who have a specified
number of dependents to obtain the number of men in
that branch/MOS/career field and grade who have the
specified number of dependents. The computer then
distributes these numbers over the years-of-service
categories by the following operation:

$$(iMSDP)^k_{g,d} \; \times \; \frac{i^k_{g,y}}{i^k_g} \; = \; (iMSDP)^k_{g,y,d}$$

Thus, the number of men for a given k and g who have
a specified number of dependents is multiplied by a
proportion equal to the inventory by k, g, and y divided by the inventory by k and g, to obtain the number of men having the specified number of dependents
by k, g, and y.

Warrant Officers

The procedure for calculating marital and dependency status of warrant officers is the same as that
described above--except that, due to lack of data,

the dependency proportions, $(DP)_{g,d}$, are the same
for each grade. The dependency rates thus vary by
grade only insofar as marital status varies by grade.

Calculation of Estimated Pay

Given the information on distribution of marital
and dependency status, it is possible to compute total pay for a force of any size (structured by grade,
years of service, and number of dependents, as specified by the user of the inventory model). As stated
above, pay is defined as the tax-equivalent total of
basic pay, quarters and subsistence allowances, and
medical, retirement, and other fringe benefits.

The computer reads in the pay by grade, years
of service, and number of dependents, denoted as
$R_{g,y,d}$ (to be distinguished from the $R_{g,y}^k$ previously
used to denote continuation). The total pay $\left(r_{g,y}^k\right)$
for each branch/MOS/career field, grade, and year of
service cell in the inventory is now calculated as
follows:

$$r_{g,y}^k = \sum_{d=1}^{5} \left[(iMSDP)_{g,y,d}^k \times R_{g,y,d} \right] + (iMS)_{g,y,0}^k \times R_{g,y,0}$$

Thus, the total pay for each cell is equal to the sum
of pay for the married men in each dependency category in that cell plus the pay of all single men in
that cell. The $r_{g,y}^k$ cells for a given k and y are
then summed for all grades to obtain r_y^k, or total pay
by branch/MOS/career field and year of service.

Total pay for the first-termers in each MOS/
branch is then calculated as

$$r_F^k = \sum_{y=1}^{3} r_y^k$$

which is the sum of pay for first-year men, second-
year men, and third-year men. Careerists are defined
as men in their fourth through thirty-first year of
service; their pay by career field/branch is calculated
as

$$r_C^k = \sum_{y=4}^{31} r_y^k$$

Having calculated total pay for the first-termers and careerists in each career field/branch, the computer obtains the corresponding inventory numbers:

$$i_F^k = \sum_{y=1}^{3} i_y^k = \text{inventory of first-termers by k}$$

$$i_C^k = \sum_{y=4}^{31} i_y^k = \text{inventory of careerists by k}$$

The weighted average wages for first-termers (Wr_F^k) and careerists (Wr_C^k) are then obtained for each k:

$$Wr_F^k = \frac{r_F^k}{i_F^k} = \frac{\text{total salaries for first-termers by k}}{\text{total number of first-termers by k}}$$

$$Wr_C^k = \frac{r_C^k}{i_C^k} = \frac{\text{total salaries for careerists by k}}{\text{total number of careerists by k}}$$

The average wage ratio of careerists to first-termers (W^k), needed as input to the enlisted effectiveness model (see Chapter 5), is calculated from the above information as

$$W^k = \frac{Wr_C^k}{Wr_F^k} = \frac{\text{average wage for careerists by k}}{\text{average wage for first-termers by k}}$$

These calculations of pay are not printed out by the computer but are stored for later use by other models. The pay information on enlisted men is later fed into the cost and relative effectiveness model

(Chapter 5). The pay information on officers and warrant officers is used by the model for estimating the cost of officers and warrant officers (Chapter 6).

The pay calculation routine would appear to be of value for Army manpower budget estimation, provided that some upward adjustments of the cost figures are made to account for additional income, such as variable reenlistment bonuses and various types of specialty pay not considered in these calculations. In addition, allowance should be made for underestimation of the actual cost of pay and allowances to the Army which results from the definition of pay used and the fact that dependents other than children are excluded from the dependency calculations (due to lack of data).

The calculation of marital and dependency status, pay, and average wages and wage ratios is an option to the user of the inventory model and does not affect the other workings of this model in any way.

DATA PREPARATION

The basic inventory model discussed in the preceding section consists of one computer program which may be run for enlisted men, warrant officers, or officers with only slight variations in program procedure. However, the efficiency gained by having a single program for all three types of personnel is offset to some extent by the requirement that the input data for each be in the same form. Since the raw data is not usually in the same form for enlisted men, warrant officers, and officers, a separate data preparation program is used to rearrange and adjust the raw data on each type of personnel into the form necessary for input to the inventory program. These data preparation procedures are discussed below.

Preparation of Data on Enlisted Men

The inventory of enlisted men for each fiscal year contains 17,298 cells (62 career fields x 9

grades x 31 years of service). This high level of
detail, which is enough to exceed the storage capa-
city of some computers, necessitates much manipulation of the data.[2]

The decision to use fiscal 1967 data on years
of service (rather than the most recent data available) was made for two reasons. First, the 1967 data
had been incorporated into the program when it was
first developed.[3] Incorporating more recent information in the course of this study would have required
very complex data manipulations which could not be
accomplished within the time limits imposed on the
study. Second, it was believed that no significant
change took place in the distribution of years of
service from fiscal 1967 to fiscal 1969.

For similar reasons, it was decided to use fiscal 1967 data on losses. Furthermore, the force simulated for this study is a hypothetical force in a
planning document. But since it is not known at which
point between fiscal 1969 and 1980 phasedown from current force levels to this hypothetical force will begin, it was assumed in simulating the inventory that
the hypothetical force (which is a constant-strength,
"peacekeeping" force) is effective immediately. This
being the case, a reasonably realistic loss rate
should be applied in calculating losses. Although
the loss rate for 1967 may not be typical of the rate
which can be anticipated in a stabilized force during
a period of peace under an all-volunteer system, the
losses experienced during the period of phasedown and
the first few years after the hypothetical force is
attained will actually be very close to recent experience. This is true not only because phasedown pro-
duces losses much heavier than usual, but also because
even after the desired strength level is reached, adjustments of the force structure continue to be made
for several years. More detailed discussion of the
loss data used in simulating the inventory is presented later in this chapter.

It should be noted that the numerical designa-
tions of the year-of-service categories read into the

computer do not correspond to those in the raw data.
The actual correspondence is the following:

Computer	Data	Designation
1	< 1	in 1st year of service
2	1	in 2nd year of service
3	2	in 3rd year of service
.	.	.
.	.	.
.	.	.
30	29	in 30th year of service
31	30+	in 31st or more year of service

Manipulation of Data

Inventory of Fiscal 1967. First, the computer
reads in the inventory of fiscal 1967, which was
coded directly from the DCSPER-199 Report. This inventory contains 63 MOSs, one more than the 62 MOSs
used in the simulation. The 63rd MOS is actually
MOS 09, which is primarily an entry MOS for trainees.
Because of the special nature of this MOS, it was decided to distribute the men in this MOS over the
other 62 MOSs in a way to be discussed later. In the
inventory model, accessions are thus added directly
into the MOSs to which, in the real world, they would
be assigned upon completion of training. If the inventory model were to simulate the real world in this
respect, the bulk of the enlisted accessions would
be added into one training MOS. This would invalidate
the primary purpose of the inventory model, which is
to generate accessions needed for each MOS.

The fiscal 1967 inventory also contains one more
year-of-service category than do simulated inventories. This 32nd year-of-service category is actually
the inventory by MOS and grade for which total years
of service are unknown in the raw data. In simulated
inventories, these unknowns are distributed over the
other 31 year-of-service categories for a given MOS
and grade by redefining the k, g, y cells, adjusting
each cell as follows:

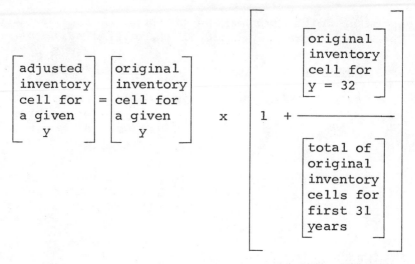

$$
\begin{bmatrix} \text{adjusted} \\ \text{inventory} \\ \text{cell for} \\ \text{a given} \\ y \end{bmatrix} = \begin{bmatrix} \text{original} \\ \text{inventory} \\ \text{cell for} \\ \text{a given} \\ y \end{bmatrix} \times \left[1 + \frac{\begin{bmatrix} \text{original} \\ \text{inventory} \\ \text{cell for} \\ y = 32 \end{bmatrix}}{\begin{bmatrix} \text{total of} \\ \text{original} \\ \text{inventory} \\ \text{cells for} \\ \text{first 31} \\ \text{years} \end{bmatrix}} \right]
$$

Thus, the original k, g, y cells for y from 1 to 31 are multiplied by a number equal to one plus a proportion equal to the number of men for whom years of service are unknown divided by the total number of men in that MOS and grade. For example, if the original inventory for a given MOS and grade is 100 men, of whom 10 are in the unknown year-of-service category, then if the number of men in the first year of service is 20, the computer calculates

$$
\begin{bmatrix} \text{adjusted} \\ \text{inventory} \\ \text{cell for} \\ y = 1 \end{bmatrix}
$$

$$= \quad 20 \times (1 + \frac{10}{100})$$

$$= \quad 20 \times (1 + .10)$$

$$= \quad 20 + 2$$

$$= \quad 22$$

Thus, the unknowns are distributed in the same proportion as the original inventory for years from 1 to 31. In the above example,

$$\frac{20}{100} = \frac{2}{10} = .2$$

<u>Separations Other than Retirements</u>. Next the computer reads in the separations that occurred during

fiscal 1967. A problem is posed by the fact that
the raw data on separations are aggregated to a lesser level of detail on years of service than is the
inventory data. The separations data contain year-
of-service categories 1, 2, 3, 4, 5, 6, 7, 8, 9, 10,
11-15, 16-20, 21 or more, and "unknown." First, the
computer distributes those separations for which
years of service are unknown in the same way that
the unknown inventory was distributed. There are 14
years-of-service categories for separations, including those which are aggregated. The 14th, or unknown, category is simply distributed according to
the proportions in the first 13 categories.

Now the separations in the 11-15, 16-20, and 21+
years-of-service categories must be disaggregated to
individual year-of-service cells. That is, the 11-15
years category, for example, must be broken down into
five categories for the 11th, 12th, 13th, 14th, and
15th year-of-service separations. The computer calculates the separations for a given MOS and grade--
for, say, 11--as follows:

$$\text{separations for } y = 11 = \text{total separations for } y = (11\text{-}15) \times \frac{\text{inventory for } y = 11}{\text{total inventory for } y = (11\text{-}15)}$$

Thus, separations are distributed according to inventory proportion. Similarly, the 16th-20th year-of-
service separations are disaggregated into five categories according to inventory proportions for those
same years, and the 21+ year separations are disaggregated into 11 categories corresponding to the 21st
through the 31st year of service.

Retirements. The raw data for retirements must
also be disaggregated in order to obtain a level of
detail corresponding to that in the inventory. Retirement data cover the following year-of-service
categories: less than 20 (lumped together) and by
individual year from 21 to 31+. The retirements for
years 21 to 31+ are read directly into computer memory. The less-than-20-year retirements, which are
almost entirely disability retirements, must be

disaggregated. For each year of service from 1
through 20, the number of retirements is calculated,
using inventory proportions. For year 1, we have

$$\begin{matrix} \text{retirements} \\ \text{for } y = 1 \end{matrix} = \begin{matrix} \text{total} \\ \text{retirements} \\ \text{for } y = (1-20) \end{matrix} \times \frac{\begin{matrix}\text{inventory}\\\text{for } y = 1\end{matrix}}{\begin{matrix}\text{total inventory}\\\text{for } y = (1-20)\end{matrix}}$$

The retirements for years 2 through 20 are then calculated. The retirements are added to separations
to obtain total losses for each k, g, y cell by redefining separations as separations plus retirements.
At this point, the computer memory contains total
losses.

Distribution of the Training MOS. The training
MOS, which is the last (63rd) MOS read into the computer, is distributed over the other 62 MOSs after
the unknown year-of-service category has been distributed. For a given grade and year of service, MOS 63
is distributed as follows:

$$\begin{bmatrix} \text{new} \\ \text{inventory} \\ \text{cell for a} \\ \text{given MOS} \end{bmatrix} = \begin{bmatrix} \text{old} \\ \text{inventory} \\ \text{cell for a} \\ \text{given MOS} \end{bmatrix} \times \left[1 + \frac{\begin{bmatrix}\text{old inventory}\\\text{cell for}\\\text{MOS 63}\end{bmatrix}}{\begin{matrix}\text{total of}\\\text{old inventory}\\\text{cells for}\\\text{first 62 MOSs}\end{matrix}} \right]$$

Thus, the old inventory cells for the first 62 MOSs
are multiplied by a number equal to one plus a proportion equal to the number of men in the training
MOS divided by the total number of men in that grade
and year of service in the other 62 MOSs. For example, if the number of men in the old inventory for
a given grade and year of service is 200, of whom 50
are in the training MOS, then if the number of men
in the first MOS is 15, the computer calculates

$$
\begin{bmatrix} \text{new} \\ \text{inventory} \\ \text{cell for} \\ \text{MOS 1} \end{bmatrix}
\begin{aligned}
&= \quad 15 \times (1 + \frac{50}{150}) \\
&= \quad 15 \times (1 + 1/3) \\
&= \quad 15 + 5 \\
&= \quad 20
\end{aligned}
$$

Continuation. Intuitively, the continuation
rate for a given k, g, y cell is equal to one minus
the loss rate for the same k, g, y cell, or

$$\text{Continuation rate} = 1 - \frac{\text{losses}}{\text{inventory}}$$

However, this is true only if losses are measured
simultaneously with the inventory, since men in the
inventory age six months, on the average, between the
point in time when they are in the inventory (June
30, 1966) and the point in time at which they are
lost (any time during fiscal 1967). For example, a
man who is near the end of his 20th year of service
in the inventory may show up as a loss in the 21st
year of service.

In order to approximate the real world more
closely, the losses for each two successive year-of-
service categories are averaged in order to correct
for the expected six-month gap between measurement
of inventory and losses. In the above example, the
losses for 20-year men would be the average of 20-
year losses plus 21-year losses. The denominator of
the loss rate (i.e., the inventory) must of course
be multiplied by two, since an average is being taken.
The continuation rate for a given k, g, y cell is thus
defined as

$$\begin{array}{c}\text{continuation} \\ \text{rate for year } y \end{array} = 1 - \frac{\left(\begin{array}{c}\text{losses for} \\ \text{year } y\end{array}\right) + \left(\begin{array}{c}\text{losses for} \\ \text{year } y + 1\end{array}\right)}{2 \times \left(\begin{array}{c}\text{inventory} \\ \text{for year } y\end{array}\right)}$$

For the final year of service (y = 31), y + 1 does
not exist, so losses for y = 32 are effectively read
in as zero. Allowances must also be made for losses
in the training MOS, or continuation rates will be
biased upward. Each continuation rate calculated
above for a given grade and year of service is therefore reduced by a factor equal to

$$\frac{\left(\begin{array}{c}\text{losses for}\\\text{training MOS}\\\text{in year } y\end{array}\right) + \left(\begin{array}{c}\text{losses for}\\\text{training MOS}\\\text{in year } y + 1\end{array}\right)}{2 \times \left(\begin{array}{c}\text{inventory for}\\\text{all MOSs for}\\\text{year } y\end{array}\right)}$$

The final definition of the continuation rate is 1 minus the loss rate minus a deduction for the training MOS.

The averaging of successive y values does not,
however, entirely solve the data problem. When the inventory preparation program for enlisted men was first
run with the modified continuation rates, many of the
rates were negative--meaning that losses exceeded inventories in those cells. This is possible because
men may have been promoted into a higher grade between the point at which they were in the inventory
and the point at which they were lost. It is also
possible that some men changed MOSs before being lost.
The only complete solution to this problem would be
to tag each man in the inventory in order to follow
the path of his migration through the forest of MOSs
grades, and years of service. Barring this solution
as infeasible, it was decided to reduce the level of
detail on continuation rates from three subscripts
to two. Three new sets of continuation rates were
calculated:

1. Continuation rate by MOS and grade (all
    years of service aggregated)

2. Continuation rate by grade and year of
    service (all MOSs aggregated)

3. Continuation rate by MOS and year of
    service (all grades aggregated).

Even at the two-subscript level of detail, each
set of rates still contained some negative numbers.
Finally, the set of rates by MOS and grade was chosen
because it had the least number of negative rates. Of
the 558 rates (9 grades x 62 MOS), only nine were negative. These negative rates were removed by having
the computer read in some reasonable value in place of
the negative rate. The rates used were .9 (for MOSs
in grade E-9), .2 (for MOSs in grade E-5), .3 (for
MOSs in grade E-4), and .8 (for MOSs in grade E-3).

Since detail on years of service is no longer
used for continuation rates, the rate for a given MOS
and grade will be the same for all 31 year-of-service
categories. However, since the inventory data reflect
a substantial correlation between grade and year of
service, there is good reason to believe that variation in continuation rates by year of service will be
reflected to a large extent in variation by grade.

The continuation rates are now in computer memory. The computer then reads the inventory of the hypothetical force simulated for this study. This inventory, which is classified by MOS and pay grade, is
then distributed by years of service, according to
the actual distribution in fiscal 1967. This inventory and the continuation rates are the final output
of the data preparation program for enlisted men and
are read into the inventory model. Simulation then
begins.

Preparation of Data on Officers

The inventory of officers for each fiscal year
contains 2,945 cells (19 branches x 5 grades x 31
years of service). First and second lieutenants are
added together because the loss data do not discrimi-
nate between them. General officers are excluded because they do not have a branch designation. The basic
inventory data on officers were obtained from the same
planning document as the basic inventory data on enlisted men. This document describes officer strength
by basic branch (k) and grade (g).[4]

Since continuation rates and distribution of years
of service for officers are calculated externally, the

officer inventory of the hypothetical force need not
be read into the computer at this point. No data
could be found on officer losses by k, g, and y simultaneously, but k, g data were available.* Thus, continuation rates for officers, like those developed
for enlisted men, vary only by k and g. The loss of
realism due to this sacrifice of detail does not appear to be sizable, again because of the close relationship between grade and year of service. While the
relationship between grade and year of service does
vary with the size of the force (as a function of the
speed of promotion), this variation is built into the
inventory simulation via the promotion routine discussed earlier in this chapter.

The problem posed by the existence of a training
MOS for enlisted men has no analogue for officers.
The y data used for officers measures years of commissioned service, and the branch assignment for an
officer is known at the point of his commissioning.

The officer inventory for the hypothetical force
(classified by k and g) is now read into the computer
and distributed over the years-of-service categories
(y) according to the distribution which existed in
fiscal 1967. Thus, the inventory is described by k,
g, and y. Continuation rates for officers are then
read into the computer.

Preparation of Data on Warrant Officers

The basic inventory data on warrant officers
were obtained from the same planning document as the
data on enlisted men and officers. The raw data on
warrant officers available for developing loss rates
and distribution of years of service were far less detailed than was desired.[5] While three-way inventory
data on k, g, and y for enlisted men and officers were
generally available, only two-way data on g, y could

_____

*Data on officer losses by k and y were dis-
covered after completion of the study. These data
could have been combined with k, g data to develop
losses by k, g, and y.

be found for warrant officers. This necessitated the
use of a separate inventory by k for warrant officers
in order to obtain estimated k, g, y cells. The data
on warrant officer losses were also less than desired,
being by grade alone.*

The inventory data for fiscal 1967 by grade and
years of service is read in. As was the case for enlisted men and officers, there is a 32nd year-of-
service category, which is the inventory by MOS and
grade for which total years of service are unknown.
For a given grade, the unknowns are distributed by
redefining the inventory cells as follows:

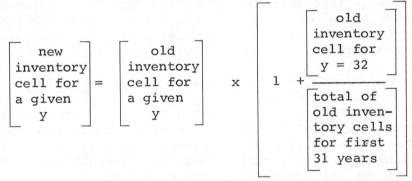

Thus, the old g, y cells for y from 1 to 31 are multiplied by a number equal to one plus a proportion equal
to the number of men for whom years of service are unknown divided by the total number of men in that grade.

The computer then reads in the inventory data on
warrant officers by grade (g) and branch (k) from the
planning document which describes the hypothetical
force to be simulated. Each of these cells (g, k) is
then distributed by grade (g) and years of service
(y) as the actual warrant officer inventory for fiscal

---

*Data on warrant officer losses by MOS were lo-
cated after completion of the study. Had they been
found earlier, they could have been aggregated into
losses by branch and combined with the losses by grade
to obtain losses by grade and branch. However, such
figures would have been simply estimates, and therefore not as reliable as the data on observed losses
used in the cases of officers and enlisted men.

1967 was distributed. Thus, for a given g, the distribution of k and y is obtained. The inventory now
contains 1,488 k, g, y cells (12 branches x 4 grades
x 31 years of service). At this point the computer
reads in the continuation rates, which are calculated
externally.

As was true of officers, there is no problem with
warrant officers analogous to the existence of a
training MOS for enlisted men. However, as discussed
earlier in this chapter, warrant officer accessions
generated by the inventory program must be added into
the second year-of-service category rather than the
first. This does not affect the data preparation program in any way. The warrant officer inventory and
continuation rates in the data preparation program are
read into the inventory model. Simulation then begins.

Loss Rates

The critical (and most difficult) element of any
model intended to project annual accession requirements is the estimate of losses and, thus, of continuation. In this study, loss rates for grade (g) and
MOS (k) cells were estimated by adding separations
(all losses other than retirements) to retirements
and dividing the total by the inventory. The data on
losses are cumulative for fiscal 1967; the inventory
is for the beginning of fiscal 1967. Continuation
rate is then defined as one minus the loss rate. Applying the continuation rate thus developed, continuation is defined as beginning strength multiplied by
the continuation rate.

In defining continuation in this manner, there
are a number of conceptual as well as practical problems. The most serious problem is the difficulty in
counting true gains and true losses. Because of the
Army's administrative procedures and personnel accounting system, recorded gains and losses in reenlistment, for example, are extremely difficult to
relate to personnel inventory. Some enlisted men reenlist prior to the end of their term of service, and
others reenlist after the end of their term of service.
This means some gains are not true gains in the current accounting period but are, in fact, gains in a

subsequent accounting period. Furthermore, some losses in a current accounting period are recovered in the
next period as gains, and hence show up in the inventory of that period. In short, true gains and losses
do not necessarily take place simultaneously within a
defined time period. Even if they do take place simultaneously, they may not actually be recorded in the
same time period because of a time lag involved in
paper work.

Because of these problems, the number of losses
recorded occasionally indicates that cumulative losses in a period exceed the inventory which existed at
the beginning of that period. This is clearly impossible. One cannot lose more than he has.

Ideally, continuation should have been defined
as beginning strength minus losses from all causes
(except losses of separatees eligible to reenlist)
minus voluntary separatees who do not reenlist even
though eligible. In this study it was impossible to
follow this definition. Some of the difficulties in
doing so have already been mentioned--namely, accounting problems in measuring both losses and inventory.
Still another difficulty stems from the Army's prac-
tice of defining eligibility for reenlistment differently at different times and, at any one time, defining it differently for different MOSs. Eligibility
is purely a matter of administrative policy and cannot be predicted. Furthermore, for the purpose of
long-run projections, losses cannot readily be broken
down into several categories, such as the following:

Involuntary Losses	Voluntary Losses
Deaths	Separatees who do not
Administrative losses	reenlist even
(those resulting from	though eligible
court-martial, etc.)	Early retirement
Early retirement because	Other voluntary losses
of disability	
Ineligibility to reenlist	
Mandatory retirement	

Projecting losses for all these categories requires
not only accurate data but also very complicated

manipulation of data based on large numbers of arbitrary assumptions. For example, in order to estimate retirement loss and voluntary loss, the number of men whose terms of service come to an end (and their distribution over years-of-service categories) must be continuously projected into the future. In addition, in estimating voluntary loss, the number of men who are ineligible to reenlist must also be projected.

The loss data used in this study are admittedly gross, but they require making fewer uncomfortable assumptions. Also, since the data are cumulative for a year, discrepancies in the accounting of gains and losses (particularly around the beginning and the end of the year) are believed to be small. If these discrepancies in data persist over the years, discrepancies in any one year are offset by those in the next.

RELATIONSHIPS TO THE OTHER MODELS

The major reason for developing the inventory model is to project the annual accessions necessary to maintain certain force requirements. In making these projections, the model generates a variety of information intended for use in the other models. The models for which such information is generated and the nature of that information are discussed briefly in Chapter 1 and in the section on calculation of pay above.

In addition, a great deal of information calculated by the inventory model is read into the model for determining the cost and relative effectiveness of enlisted men (see Chapter 5). The following information, most of which is not actually printed out by the inventory model, is fed into the enlisted effectiveness model where it is printed out for each year t of each scenario from $t = 1$ to $t = T$.

$a_{k,t}$ = accessions by MOS/branch ($A_{k,t}$ in Chapter 5)

$s_{k,t}$ = surpluses by MOS/branch

$f_{k,t}$ = proportion who are first-termers in each MOS/branch ($1 - \gamma_{k,t}$ in Chapter 5)

$n_{k,t}$ = proportion of first-termers who are in first year of service in each MOS/branch

$z_{k,t}$ = proportion of first-termers who are in second year of service in each MOS/branch

$I_{k,t}$ = inventory for each MOS/branch

$w_{k,t}$ = wage ratio of careerists to first-termers in each MOS/branch ($\omega_{k,t}$ in Chapter 5)

$w_{f,k,t}$ = weighted average of pay for first-termers in each MOS/branch ($r_{f,k,t}$ in Chapter 5)

$w_{c,k,t}$ = weighted average of pay for careerists in each MOS/branch ($r_{c,k,t}$ in Chapter 5)

f_t = proportion of total first-termers ($1 - \gamma_t$ in Chapter 5)

n_t = proportion of total first-termers who are in the first year of service

z_t = proportion of total first-termers who are in the second year of service

I_t = total inventory

RESULTS AND INTERPRETATIONS

The tables on the following pages summarize the results of the run of the inventory models made for this study. As explained earlier, the size and structure of the force used to begin the simulation

were those of a hypothetical force deemed adequate
for "peacekeeping." This force was specified for use
in this study by the Army. The period simulated was
fiscal 1969-80.

Table 2 summarizes the annual accessions of enlisted men, officers, and warrant officers projected
by the models to be necessary to maintain this force.
Table 3 focuses on enlisted men, showing beginning
strength, continuing strength, and required accessions
for each fiscal year of the simulation period. Table
4 shows the projected number of Negro enlisted men in
the force described in Table 3. Table 5 presents
comparable projections of the number of non-Negro enlisted men in this force.

TABLE 2

Annual Accessions to Active Army Strength,
Fiscal Years 1969-80

Fiscal Year	Enlisted Men	Officers	Warrant Officers	Total
1969	350,769	53,568	1,860	406,197
1970	312,501	20,496	1,201	334,198
1971	322,139	20,859	1,300	344,298
1972	322,324	21,023	1,300	344,647
1973	322,351	21,228	1,300	344,879
1974	322,373	21,389	1,307	345,069
1975	322,363	21,511	1,320	345,194
1976	322,393	21,620	1,321	345,334
1977	322,366	21,712	1,315	345,393
1978	322,344	21,798	1,321	345,463
1979	322,339	21,861	1,326	345,526
1980	322,303	21,905	1,332	345,540

Source: Output of the run of the inventory
models made for this study.

As discussed in the section on loss rates, the
projected accessions shown in Table 2 are subject to
the limitation that fiscal 1967 losses were used in
calculating the continuation rates on which they are
based. To the extent that fiscal 1967 was not a typical year in terms of continuation, the accessions
will, of course, be affected. It will be noticed that
the number of accessions projected for each year is
very stable. To some extent, the combined effect of
using constant continuation rates and maintaining the
force at a constant strength throughout the simulation may overstate the degree of stability. However,
experience has demonstrated that in periods of stable
total strength, changes in overall continuation rates
are small and annual accessions vary only mildly.
This was the case, for example, in the early 1960's
(with the exception of the period of the Cuban missile
crisis).

TABLE 3

Overall Inventory of Enlisted Men,
Fiscal Years 1969-80

Fiscal Year	Beginning Strength	Continuations	Accessions
1969	902,141	523,575	350,769
1970	874,344	546,392	312,501
1971	858,893	536,495	322,139
1972	858,634	536,291	322,324
1973	858,615	536,264	322,351
1974	858,615	536,242	322,373
1975	858,615	536,252	322,363
1976	858,615	536,222	322,393
1977	858,615	536,249	322,366
1978	858,615	536,271	322,344
1979	858,615	536,276	322,339
1980	858,615	536,312	322,303

Source: Output of the run of the inventory
model for enlisted men made for this study.

TABLE 4

Inventory of Negro Enlisted Men,
Fiscal Years 1969-80

Fiscal Year	Beginning Strength[a]	Continuations[b]	Accessions[c]
1969	114,571	70,392	53,668
1970	124,060	76,173	47,813
1971	123,985	76,127	49,287
1972	125,414	77,004	49,316
1973	126,320	77,560	49,320
1974	126,880	77,904	49,323
1975	127,227	78,117	49,322
1976	127,439	78,248	49,326
1977	127,574	78,331	49,322
1978	127,653	78,379	49,319
1979	127,698	78,407	49,318
1980	127,725	78,423	49,312

[a]For fiscal 1969 beginning strength, 12.7 percent of overall beginning enlisted strength (as it appears in Table 3) was assumed to be Negro. This was the actual Negro participation rate as of December 31, 1968.

[b]The loss rate was calculated by dividing the number of Negro separations (of both first-termers and careerists in the Regular Army) by the total number of Negro enlisted men as of December 31, 1968. The continuation rate (.614) was obtained by subtracting the loss rate from 1. This continuation rate was used as a constant for fiscal years 1969-80.

[c]It was assumed that 15.3 percent of the total number of enlistees are Negro. This percentage was derived from the Army Sample Survey of Military Personnel (Enlistees), approximately April, 1969.

Source: Negro participation and continuation rates were derived from Statistical Reports on Military Personnel Strength and Turnover by Race (U), RCS: DDM-A-626 as of December 31, 1968, RCS:DDM-A-626.

TABLE 5

Inventory of Non-Negro Enlisted Men,
Fiscal Years 1969-80

Fiscal Year	Beginning Strength	Continuations	Accessions
1969	787,570	453,183	297,101
1970	750,284	470,219	264,688
1971	734,908	460,368	272,852
1972	733,220	459,287	273,008
1973	732,295	458,704	273,031
1974	731,735	458,338	273,050
1975	731,388	458,135	273,041
1976	731,176	457,974	273,067
1977	731,041	457,918	273,044
1978	730,962	457,892	273,025
1979	730,917	457,869	273,021
1980	730,890	457,889	272,991

Source: Derived by subtracting the figures
for Negro enlisted strength in Table 4 from overall
enlisted strength in Table 3. That is to say, non-
Negro strength is the residual.

All the inventory estimates (for enlisted men,
warrant officers, and officers) were made under the
assumption that the size of the Army is reduced to
the hypothetical "peacekeeping" level immediately.
However, the continuation rates used in making these
estimates are current ones--specifically, fiscal 1967.
These rates obviously do not reflect the impact of
changes in pay policy necessary for maintaining an
all-volunteer force. In all probability, the continuation rates experienced by an all-volunteer force
would be higher. Thus, with proper pay and additional incentives, the annual accessions required for
this force under an all-volunteer system would, in the
long run, be lower than those shown in the tables of
this section. This point is discussed further in
Chapter 4.

NOTES

1. The sources of data for these calculations
are "Survey Estimates of Marital Status and Dependents
of Army Male Personnel," OPO Recurring Sample Survey
(August 31, 1960); and "Tax Equivalent and Tax Advan-
tages of Military Pay and Allowances" (OASD [Manpower]
Actuarial Office, 1969).

2. Raw data on the inventory of enlisted men
was obtained from the following documents: for distribution years of service, "Enlisted Personnel by
Years of Active Federal Military Service, Primary MOS
and Grade," from DCSPER-199 Report (Part III) for
fiscal 1967; for distribution of two-digit MOS and
grade, a hypothetical force structure deemed adequate
for "peacekeeping," which was developed by the Department of the Army for a 1969 planning document.

Raw data on losses of enlisted men were obtained from "Cumulative Enlisted Separations, Summary
for FY 1967," Part I--Active Army Enlisted Personnel:
Section C--Retirements by Grade, Active Federal Service, and Primary MOS; Section D--Separations by Grade,
Active Federal Service, and Primary MOS.

3. K. H. Kim et al., An Army 75 Personnel Procurement Concept (Battelle Memorial Institute, July
31, 1968). For the Department of the Army, Contract
DAHC 19 67 C 0031.

4. The raw data on officers used for deriving
loss rates and years of service distribution are obtained from "RA and OTRA Commissioned Officers by Basic
Branch and Years of Active Federal Commissioned Service" (for each grade), from OPD STAT-7 Report as of
June 30, 1967; and "Cumulative Officer Losses by Branch
and Grade," from DEXSO-8 Report as of June 30, 1967.

5. The following were used as raw data on war-
rant officers: "Current Actual Strength by Years of
Active Federal Service, Grade, and Category (RA and
OTRA)," from COPO-11 Report as of June 30, 1967;
"Current Actual Strength by Branch and MOS," from OPD
STAT-7 Report as of June 30, 1967; and "Cumulative
Losses by Cause and Grade," from DCSPER-46, COPO-13,
and DEXSO-8 Reports as of June 30, 1967.

CHAPTER **3** THE CIVILIAN
MANPOWER POOL
MODEL

The civilian manpower pool model was designed
to project the number of men available for military
service under different military manpower procurement policies. Briefly stated, the task was to define the projected male population, aged 16 through
26, of three racial groups (white, Negro, others) for
each fiscal year from 1969 to 1980, for each of the
five Army recruiting districts in terms of educational attainment, marital status, and whether or not
they have children. Had all the necessary information been available for each state, the task would
have been a simple reclassification of the figures
by Army recruiting districts. The data available,
however, did not permit this. Therefore, the major
effort of this segment of the study was devoted to
selecting and organizing a consistent set of statistical information and to developing missing but necessary information on the basis of certain assumptions.

The estimates developed rely heavily on a series
of reports published by the Bureau of the Census entitled Current Population Reports: Population
Estimates; this series includes both current data
and projections. Relying on the Bureau's published
studies was considered preferable to using projections from a number of sources--largely because relying on a single source enhances consistency and permits greater maneuverability of the data. Only when
results of the Bureau's studies were not available
in published form were independent judgments introduced.

Assumptions, methodological details, and data are all described below. Extracts from the computer printout of the model appear in Appendix A.*

BASIC POPULATION

By Age

The information necessary for projecting the total male population for 1969-1980 is available in the Bureau of Census publication Current Population Reports: Population Estimates, Series P-25, Nos. 381 and 388. Table 14 of No. 381, "Estimates and Projections of the Population of the United States Under 40 Years Old, by Single Years of Age and Sex: 1966 to 1985," gives bench mark figures for projections of the male population of the United States under 40 years of age by single years of age for 1966, 1970, 1975, 1980, and 1985.** Four different estimates of population are included in this table; these estimates are based on different assumptions on population growth which imply four different assumptions on fertility trends. Of the four estimates, Series D was selected for this study. Series D is consistent with the assumption that the level of completed fertility will be 2,450 children per 1,000 women (for cohorts of women who reach the childbearing age of 14 years after July, 1965). This is the most conservative of the four assumptions on fertility and is equivalent, historically, to the experience of cohorts of women born in 1900-05. Except for the cohorts of 1905-15, whose childbearing ages coincided with the

---

*The extracts of the civilian manpower pool model which appear in Appendix A include men who were in military service or had completed military service by the beginning of fiscal 1969 and men classified by the Selective Service System as not qualified for military service (4F) or qualified only in time of war or national emergency (1Y).

**The figures in this table relate to July 1 and include members of the armed forces abroad.

severe years of the Depression, the cohorts of 1900-
05 showed the lowest fertility in this century.

Using these bench mark figures, the rest of the
task was simply to interpolate between pairs of bench
mark years. For each age cohort, the aging was accomplished through use of a constant exponential rate
--that is to say, at a compound rate which validated
the two bench mark points. By this process, the total male population by single years of age was derived
for every year between 1969 and 1980.

By Racial Group

A set of projections for the nonwhite population
consistent with this projection of total male population was obtained from Table 6 of Current Population
Reports: Population Estimates, Series P-25, No. 388:
"Estimates and Projections of the Nonwhite Population
of the United States, by Age and Sex: 1960 to 1990."
However, this table gives projected figures only for
multiple age groups. In order to develop a projection by single years of age, the Bureau's single-age
population estimate of nonwhites up to 1968 was used,
and an estimate of single-year age groups for each of
the ensuing years was obtained by the cohort-aging
method.

The residual derived by deducting the projected
number of nonwhite males from the projected total
number of males is regarded as the white male population.

There is no satisfactory guide for projecting
the further division of the nonwhite population between "Negroes" and "others." The average relationship observed in 1965-67 was assumed to prevail over
the projection period.

By Army Recruiting District

This projection by racial group of the total number of young men in the United States aged 16 through
26 serves as the basic guide to which state-by-state
projections should theoretically conform. The future

trend of population size and racial composition on
the state level depends not only on the fertility of
each race but also on interstate migration. The
Bureau of the Census projects state population trends
on the basis of two different assumptions. The projection in Series I assumes that the pattern of interstate migration observed in 1955-60, conditioned by
net interstate migration in 1960-65, will prevail in
the near future. The projection in Series II assumes
that interstate migration will disappear over the
next 50 years. Implicit in the second assumption,
of course, is the fact that differing conditions among
the states which induce interstate migration at present will not be important in half a century. Since
this second assumption seemed plausible, Series II-D
in Table 18 of Current Population Reports: Population
Estimates, Series P-25, No. 388, was selected for this
study. Table 18 is titled "Projections of the Population of States, by Broad Age Groups: 1965 and
1975." The age group of 5 through 24 was selected
and its population trend was estimated up to 1980,
assuming a linear trend, with 1965 and 1975 as bench
mark figures.

     Trends in state population are of interest to
this study only because they help in projecting population trends for Army recruiting districts. Accord-
ingly, the projection of geographical trends in population was performed after grouping the states into
recruiting districts. Necessary adjustments based on
population distribution within a state were made for
those states which are divided into more than one recruiting district.

     Unfortunately, the projection of state population
in Table 18 does not distinguish among the races. For
information on the nonwhite population it was necessary to supplement Table 18 with Table 9 of Current
Population Reports: Population Estimates, Series P-
25, No. 375, which is titled "Projections of the Nonwhite Population, by Age, for Selected States: 1975
and 1985." To maintain consistency with Table 18,
Series II-D and age group 5 through 24 were selected
from Table 9. However, since Table 9 includes only
those states which had a nonwhite population of

250,000 or more in 1960, it was necessary to intro-
duce an assumption to account for states which are
excluded from the table because of the small size of
their population or the small proportion of nonwhites.

It was assumed that the proportion of nonwhites
within a recruiting district is equal to the average
proportion of nonwhites observed in those states in
the same district which had a nonwhite population of
more than 250,000 in 1960. A recruiting district
which includes many states with a high proportion of
nonwhites is obviously subject to the least degree of
approximation, since projections of nonwhite population are available from the Bureau's study for practically all the states in the district. In a district
in which the nonwhite population constitutes a relatively insignificant proportion, there may be danger
of overestimation. However, careful examination of
this possibility dispels concern. First, the weight
of the population in those states for which nonwhite
population projections are not available is relatively small compared with the total population of the
recruiting districts to which they belong; second,
the proportion of nonwhites in these states is not
greatly different from the proportion in adjacent
states for which a projection of nonwhite population
is available. For instance, in 1960 the population
of the state of New York, which belongs to the First
Army Recruiting District, included 1,495,000 nonwhites.
This was 8.5 percent of the state's total population
--a percentage not greatly different from that in
Massachusetts, a state in the First District for which
no projection of nonwhite population is available.

Adjustments for Statistical Discrepancies

After the population trend up to 1980 was established for whites and nonwhites in each recruiting
district, adjustments were made for statistical discrepancies from the national total and the district
totals for ages 16-24 were broken down into single-
year age groups. The adjustment for statistical discrepancies was required for two major reasons. The
first and obvious reason is that the population figures for each district include both men and women,

while the national projection was of men only. Second, the district figures do not include members of the armed forces abroad, while the national projections do. Two assumptions were therefore introduced: that male-female ratios are identical in all recruiting districts and that each district's representation in the armed forces abroad is in essentially the same proportion as that district's population to the nation's total population.

Under these assumptions, all that is required for adjustment of statistical discrepancies is to reduce the projected population of each recruiting district in equal proportions so as to make the total population of all the districts conform to the total male population projected for the nation as a whole.

Distribution of District Projections by Single Years of Age

The projections of male population in each district thus attained are cumulative of age groups 5-24. For distribution by single years of age, it was assumed that the national distribution by single years of age for this age group is applicable to all districts. Although this assumption may not be valid for comparison on the state level for each age group (e.g., Florida would have more older age groups than New York), it need not apply to all age groups, but only to the group aged 5-24, in which variation among states is less than variation in other age groups.

The age group of interest for this study, of course, is the group aged 16-26. Thus, the age group of 25 and 26 must be added to the estimate of 16-24-year-olds. This was accomplished by establishing an average relationship between the age groups of 16-24 and of 25 and 26 on the national level, then applying the relationship to the population of 16-24-year-olds projected for each recruiting district. This is clearly not an ideal approximation, but given the limitations of the data, it was thought to be best.

CHARACTERISTICS OF THE YOUNG MALE POPULATION

At this point, the population projections for each district derived from the projection model are devoid of all population characteristics but race. Yet if the model is to be a useful tool in military manpower procurement, it must provide more information than mere population figures. That is, the projection must include information on expected future development in several important population characteristics. Many characteristics have a bearing on accessions and the composition of the armed forces, but three were selected for consideration in this study because of their primary importance: educational attainment, marital status, and dependents.

There is abundant literature describing population with a single and isolated characteristic. With relative ease, population trends can be described in terms of educational attainment or marital status or dependents. But there is no study which satisfactorily describes how trends in these three population characteristics will develop simultaneously. The task is much more complicated than superimposing separate population studies of single characteristics on a given sex and age group. Such methodology would be valid only if each of the characteristics were independent of the others. The fact is almost the opposite. For instance, marital status has a significant bearing on decisions about education and, at the same time, educational status seriously influences the decision to marry. The relationship between marital status and dependents is almost axiomatic. The interdependent nature of these characteristics presents extreme complications for statistical estimation. In fact, the complexity increases by geometric progression with the introduction of each additional characteristic to the projection model.

However, the essential features of the model for projecting population characteristics are quite simple. A table is constructed which shows how the male population of a specified age and racial group in a specified recruiting district will be distributed in terms of educational attainment, marital status, and

dependents in a specified year. In order to con-
struct this table, matrices of ratios which cross-
classify characteristics are constructed for each
age and racial group from 1969 to 1980. The age
groups, of course, are expressed in single years of
age, from 16 through 26.

A typical population table for the male population of a specified age, racial group, and recruiting district in a specified year is shown below.

	Married		Unmarried
	With depen- dents	Without depen- dents	

Enrolled:
  Below college
  In college
  Graduate and
    professional
 	
Not enrolled:
  High school graduate
  Not high school
    graduate			

With relevant figures filled in, this table provides information on the number of young men with
specific population characteristics.

Marital Status, Dependents

As can be seen in the table above, marital status is projected in two classifications. The "married" classification consists of males with their
spouses present. Men who are widowed or are sepa-
rated or divorced from their wives are treated as
"unmarried," as are those who have never married.

Only married males with their spouses present
are presumed to have dependents. Clearly, reality
can be contrary to this assumption. Yet the

assumption is not so counter to fact as might appear
at first glance. First, the assumption is applied
only to men who are 16-26 years old. The great majority of men under 20 years of age are not married,
and those who marry before the age of 26 are likely
to have a limited number of married years behind
them. Therefore, the possibility of their losing a
spouse through separation, divorce, or other cause
is not great. It is even less likely that a spouse
will be lost after the arrival of offspring. Even
when this is the case, however, because of the nature
of civil law in the United States, the offspring are
likely to be dependents of the woman rather than the
man. In fact, it is probably for these reasons that
no published statistics on the dependents of unmarried people exist.

Educational Attainment

Educational attainment is projected in two major
classifications: "enrolled" and "not enrolled."
These classifications are then subdivided to indicate
each person's last year of school enrollment. For
those who were not enrolled in any educational insti-
tution at the time of the 1960 census, the basis for
classification is their highest education attainment.

The "not-enrolled" classification has only two
sub-classifications: "high school graduate" and
"not high school graduate." The latter classification implies that high school dropouts are grouped
with elementary school graduates and dropouts. The
classification "high school graduates" includes high
school graduates, college dropouts and, in theory,
college graduates. For the age group under consideration, however, the number of people who have received college degrees and are out of school is relatively small.

Distribution of Characteristics by Racial Group, Single Years of Age

Population data with all three population characteristics needed for this study are difficult to
find; the difficulty is compounded when the data

sought must have racial as well as single-age breakdowns.

The basic data for these breakdowns came from
the published results of the 1960 population census.
Specifically, Tables 8 and 14 of the School Enrollment volume (PC(2)-5A) and Table 168 of the U.S. Summary volume (PC(1)-1D) were most useful. Table 8
shows school enrollment status for the group aged 16-
34 of the population, divided into marital and dependency categories; it is titled "Marital Status, Presence of Own Children, and Labor Force Status, by
Whether or not Enrolled in College and Year of College
in Which Enrolled--Persons 16 to 34 Years Old, by Age,
Color, and Sex, for the United States: 1960." Its
weakness is that the information is available for
several broad multi-age groupings and that the population "not enrolled" is combined into one class without showing its educational attainment.

Table 14 provides the missing information on educational attainment of those not enrolled in school.
It is titled "Family Status by Educational Attainment
of Those not Enrolled in School--Persons 14 to 24
Years Old, by Age, Color, and Sex, for the United
States, by Type of Residence: 1960." Yet this table,
too, is based on multi-age groups. The status of
school enrollment and nonenrollment by single years
of age is shown in Table 168, which is titled "Year
of School in Which Enrolled by Single Years of Age,
Color, and Sex for the United States: 1960." It is
these statistics that enabled transforming multiple-
age groups to single-year age groups based on educational characteristics.

The information necessary to transform figures
on marital status from multiple-age groups to single-
year age groups was derived from Table 11 of Current
Population Reports: Population Estimates, Series
P-25, No. 388: "Estimates and Projections of the
Total and Single Resident Population of the United
States, by Age and Sex: 1960 to 1985." Interpolation was made on the basis of a compound growth rate.
Then the number of people with dependents was assumed
to be proportional to the number of people married in
each single-year age group.

Extrapolation of Trends

Of the three population characteristics dealt with in the projection model, the most drastic changes during the 1960's have occurred in educational attainment--and the 1970's are likely to witness further changes. (Judging from available studies, expected changes in marital and dependency status of the age group considered in this study are relatively insignificant.) In order to determine the past rate of change in education, statistical tables comparable to those for 1960 were constructed for 1968. The Bureau of the Census provided the required data on educational attainment by race in 1968. These 1968 population data based on education characteristics were further transformed into the desired population tables on the assumption that the distribution of marital and dependency status observed in 1960 is also applicable in 1968.

The two 1960 tables (enrolled and not enrolled by racial group, age, and marital and dependency status) and the two comparable tables constructed for 1968 express population in absolute numbers. These tables were transferred into matrices of ratios by dividing the figures in each cell by the total population in a given age group. The matrices were then grouped by racial categories.

At this point, the ratio tables are useful for showing the relative importance of a subgroup with distinctive population characteristics to the total population of a given age. For instance, they show what proportion of the total population of white 20-year-olds is single, without dependents, and enrolled in college.

In addition, since every cell is expressed in ratios, it is now possible to compare 1960 and 1968 for the purpose of finding trends without being hindered by the absolute increase in population during this period. As indicated previously, from 1960 to 1968 a marked decline was observed in "not enrolled, not high school graduates"--regardless of other population characteristics. This decline was, of course,

counterbalanced by an increase in general educational
level in other cells.

The trends in population characteristics from
1960 to 1968 thus observed were used as the basis for
extrapolating to 1980. So drastic was the increase
in general educational level in the 1960's that any
attempt to employ linear projection was clearly in-
appropriate. As an example, if the nonenrolled population of 16-26-year-olds with less than a full high
school education continues to decrease in the 1970's
at the same rate observed in the 1960's, then long
before 1980 the entire population with this characteristic will disappear. A general trend bridging
1960 to 1968 and then extending up to 1980 clearly
implied a curvilinear form. The trend assumed in our
model takes a curvature progressing asymptotically
toward 1980.

Distribution of Characteristics by District

Estimates of population with the desired characteristics in terms of absolute number are obtained
by multiplying the projected basic population of each
district by the appropriate matrix of ratios of population characteristics (by race). It was obviously
impossible to design a separate set of matrices each
of which contains all characteristics for each recruiting district. A set designed for the nation as a
whole was employed for all district projections.

OPTIONS IN THE MODEL

Since the model is intended to be useful for
military manpower planning, it was designed to permit
reducing the gross manpower estimates for each recruiting district by the following numbers:

1. The number of men who were either in
    military service or had completed mili-
    tary service by the beginning of fiscal
    year 1969

2. The number of Selective Service regis-
    trants classified as not qualified for

                    military service (4F) or qualified only
                    in time of war or national emergency (1Y).

     It should be emphasized that these subtractions
are options in the model which may be exercised at
the discretion of the user.*

     Subtraction of Servicemen and Veterans

     In order to estimate the number of men with no
prior military service at the beginning of fiscal
year 1969, it is necessary to estimate the number who
were either in service (servicemen) or had completed
service (veterans) by the beginning of fiscal 1969.
The first step was to obtain the number of men in
each age group in each Army recruiting district at
the beginning of fiscal 1969. This analysis was conducted separately for draftees (inductees) and for
enlistees with no prior service (NPS)--that is, for
men who enlisted voluntarily.

     The next step was to estimate the number of
draftees who were either servicemen or veterans aged
17-26 at the end of fiscal 1968 (which is the same
as the beginning of fiscal 1969). It was necessary
to begin with 17-year-old volunteer draftees** in
1960, since they were 26-year-old servicemen or veterans in fiscal 1969. The draftees aged 17 in service in fiscal 1960 were then aged one year and added
to the draftees aged 18 in fiscal 1961, and so on.[1]

     A similar analysis was conducted to obtain the
age distribution of NPS enlistees--although in this
case some data had to be manufactured.[2] First, a
percentage distribution of men aged 17-26 was obtained from the detailed data for fiscal 1966 and
1967. Since only median ages were available for
earlier years (fiscal 1960-65), percentage distributions of age for each of these years and for fiscal

_____

     *Two runs of the civilian manpower pool models
were made for this study (one including 1Ys, 4Fs,
servicemen, and veterans; the other, excluding them).

     **Seventeen-year-olds can volunteer for the draft.

1968 were obtained by applying the fiscal 1966-67 percentage distribution around the median ages in fiscal
1960-65 and 1968. The percentage distributions for
fiscal 1960-65 were then applied to the total NPS enlistments in each of those years to obtain the number
of enlistees of each age in each year. From this
point, the procedure is the same as that used for in-
ductees--that is, the 17-year-olds who enlisted in
fiscal 1960 are aged and added to the 18-year-olds
who enlisted in fiscal 1961, and so on. An upward
adjustment is made in each year to account for the
number of reservists who transferred to active duty
status, using the same age distributions used for
enlistees.

The age-specific distribution of enlistees who
were servicemen or veterans at the end of fiscal 1968
is thus obtained, and is added to the same distribution of draftees to obtain the total age-specific distribution of enlisted servicemen and veterans aged 17-
24 at the beginning of fiscal 1969. This distribution
is then proportioned to the Selective Service classifications, by recruiting district, for men in service
(enlisted, commissioned, and inducted) and veterans as
of June 30, 1968. This permits exclusion of officers
as well as enlisted men. Since warrant officers enter
the Army as enlisted men, they, too, are excluded by
this process. The fiscal 1968 age groups are then
aged one year and added to the age-specific accessions
for fiscal 1969 in order to estimate the number of servicemen and veterans in each recruiting district who
are aged 17 through 26 at the beginning of fiscal 1969.
This number is then subtracted from the total population of the appropriate district.

Subtraction of Selective Service Registrants Classified 1Y and 4F

The civilian manpower available in each recruiting district per fiscal year can be further reduced
by the number of men who, on a historical basis, can
be expected to be classified 1Y or 4F by the Selective Service.

This number was determined by dividing the states,
the District of Columbia, and the three territories

(Guam, Puerto Rico, and the Virgin Islands) into the
five Army recruiting districts effective July 1, 1969.
On the basis of this division, the total number of
Selective Service registrants classified, the number
classified 1Y, and the number classified 4F per district were calculated for each fiscal year from 1963
to 1969 (from data contained in the Annual Report of
the Director of Selective Service). Then the sum of
classified registrants, the sum of those classified
1Y, and the sum of those classified 4F over the
period 1963-69 were calculated for each recruiting
district. Once these sums were established, the ratio of 1Ys in each district to the total number classified in that district and the ratio of 4Fs in each
district to the total number classified in that district were calculated. The ratios established according to this method were as follows:

	1Ys	4Fs
First District*	5.8	6.5
Third District	5.6	13.2
Fourth District	8.5	7.5
Fifth District	6.3	5.7
Sixth District	5.9	6.5

At this point, the ratios for each district were
applied against the civilian manpower pool in that
district for each fiscal year from 1969 to 1980.
Thus, the total number of men available for military
service in each district per fiscal year was reduced
by the number of men in each district who, on the
basis of the historically derived ratios, can be expected to be classified 1Y and 4F.

RESULTS AND INTERPRETATIONS

The output of the civilian manpower pool model
offers the user a wide range of information on the
composition of the civilian manpower pool which it
projects to be available for military service.

---

*There is no Second Army Recruiting District.

Although the population characteristics matrix for each racial group is constructed by simultaneous consideration of three elements, the projected population with any single characteristic or with a combination of any two characteristics can be determined with ease because of the form of the output. For example, for a given age and racial group in a given recruiting district, it is possible to estimate the number of men who are married, have children, and have at least a college education. If it is not important to know whether these men have children, this classification may be dropped altogether, and the estimated number of men in the district who are married and have at least a college education can then be tabulated. Still another estimate of population can be generated by dropping consideration of marital status. Or the user may wish to have information on the young male population of the country as a whole or on all racial groups in a single district or on all age groups in a single racial group.

In addition, the user may exercise control over the detailed output of the model by inserting accumulation control cards which tell the computer which men are to be considered available and unavailable. For example, it might be specified that, given a net pool of "available" men, "desired" manpower is defined as those men who have completed high school and are single or married without children.

Tables 6 and 7 are examples of controlled results of the model. Table 6 shows the projected number of 18-26-year-old civilian males per fiscal year (to 1980) from the model which excludes 1Ys, 4Fs, servicemen, and veterans. Table 7 summarizes the projected number of civilian males aged 17-20 who are not enrolled in school, who are fully employed, and who are available and qualified for military service in each fiscal year to 1980; this projection, too, is based on the model which excludes 1Ys, 4Fs servicemen, and veterans. Note that in Table 7 the projected numbers of "fully employed" males aged 17-20, not enrolled in school, are based on assumed unemployment rates of .15 and .10; the projected numbers of "qualified," fully employed males aged 17-20,

TABLE 6

Summary of 18-26-Year-Olds from Civilian Manpower
Pool Model, Excluding 1Ys, 4Fs,
Veterans, and Servicemen,
Fiscal Years 1969-80

Fiscal Year	Total	White	Negro	Other
1969	10,114,303	8,846,160	1,159,795	108,348
% of Total		87.46	11.47	1.07
1970	10,447,616	9,125,809	1,208,896	112,911
% of Total		87.35	11.57	1.08
1971	10,910,027	9,512,612	1,278,419	118,996
% of Total		87.19	11.72	1.09
1972	11,393,975	9,919,644	1,348,530	125,801
% of Total		87.06	11.84	1.10
1973	11,931,474	10,397,965	1,402,764	130,745
% of Total		87.15	11.76	1.10
1974	12,082,902	10,466,271	1,478,516	138,115
% of Total		86.62	12.24	1.14
1975	12,353,967	10,682,274	1,528,846	142,847
% of Total		86.47	12.38	1.16
1976	12,631,812	10,910,919	1,573,947	146,946
% of Total		86.38	12.46	1.16
1977	12,931,360	11,159,957	1,620,190	151,213
% of Total		86.30	12.53	1.17
1978	13,187,763	11,367,991	1,664,435	155,337
% of Total		86.20	12.62	1.18
1979	13,454,635	11,570,369	1,723,451	160,815
% of Total		86.00	12.81	1.20
1980	13,630,745	11,697,359	1,768,061	165,325
% of Total		85.82	12.97	1.21

Source: Table is based on output of civilian manpower pool model.

TABLE 7

Summary of Fully Employed Males, Aged 17-20, Not Enrolled in School,
Available and Qualified for Military Service, Fiscal Years 1969-80
(in thousands)

Fiscal Year	(1) Total Available Males	(2) Total Available Males not Enrolled in School	(3) No. in Col. 2 Who Are Employed (.85)a	(4) No. in Col. 2 Who Are Employed (.90)b	(5) No. in Col. 3 Who Are Qualified for Military Service (.60)c	(6) No. in Col. 3 Who Are Qualified for Military Service (.70)c	(7) No. in Col. 4 Who Are Qualified for Military Service (.60)c	(8) No. in Col. 4 Who Are Qualified for Military Service (.70)c
1969	4,955	1,696	1,442	1,527	865	1,009	916	1,069
1970	5,098	1,712	1,455	1,541	873	1,018	924	1,078
1971	5,283	1,763	1,499	1,587	899	1,049	952	1,111
1972	5,473	1,820	1,547	1,638	928	1,083	983	1,147
1973	5,640	1,880	1,598	1,692	959	1,118	1,015	1,184
1974	5,770	1,920	1,632	1,728	979	1,142	1,037	1,209
1975	5,887	1,963	1,668	1,766	1,001	1,168	1,060	1,236
1976	5,967	1,992	1,693	1,793	1,016	1,185	1,076	1,255
1977	6,046	2,023	1,720	1,821	1,032	1,204	1,092	1,275
1978	6,136	2,043	1,736	1,838	1,042	1,215	1,103	1,287
1979	6,183	2,067	1,757	1,860	1,054	1,230	1,116	1,302
1980	6,196	2,080	1,768	1,872	1,061	1,238	1,123	1,311

aBased on an assumed unemployment rate of .15.

bBased on an assumed unemployment rate of .10.

cBased on qualification rates at Armed Forces Entrance and Examining Stations, which historically have ranged from .6 to .7.

Source: The first two columns abstracted from the civilian manpower pool model excluding 1Ys, 4Fs, servicemen, and veterans.

not enrolled in school, are based on qualification
rates at Armed Forces Entrance and Examining Stations,
which historically have ranged from .6 to .7.

The output of the civilian manpower pool model
is directly useful for estimation of the supply of
enlisted volunteers and the cost of an all-volunteer
military service. The population in Table 6, for example, is equivalent to the population variable used
in this report for estimating the number of young men
who would volunteer for military service under an all-
volunteer system. The population in Table 7 is rough-
ly equivalent to the population used by Altman in his
estimation of the supply of enlisted volunteers[3] and
by Fisher-Kim in this report. Fisher's own estimate[4]
is based on a population which can be obtained from
the civilian manpower pool model by accumulating the
number of males 17-20 years old including 1Ys and
4Fs but excluding servicemen. The usefulness of the
manpower projection is explained in more detail in
Chapter 4, in the course of discussing the supply of
enlisted volunteers.

The user is cautioned that beginning with fiscal
1969, annual accessions to all the services must be
subtracted from the projected civilian manpower pool.

NOTES

1. The time-series on draftee age distribution
was obtained from the report titled "Age and Status of
Inductees, United States" (monthly), Statistics Section, Research and Statistics, National Headquarters,
Selective Service System, covering fiscal 1960-68.

2. The basic sources of data on the age distribution of enlistees were "NPS Enlistments by Year of
Birth," Directorate of Procurement Policy, OASD (Manpower), fiscal 1966 and 1967; and "Median Age of Enlistees and Inductees, FY 1954-1966," from Reference
Materials from the Department of Defense Study of the
Draft (July, 1966).

3. Stuart H. Altman, "Earnings, Unemployment, and the Supply of Enlisted Volunteers," The Journal of Human Resources (1969), Vol. 4, No. 1, pp. 38-59.

4. Anthony C. Fisher, "The Cost of the Draft and the Cost of Ending the Draft," American Economic Review, Vol. LIX, No. 3, June, 1969.

CHAPTER **4** THE SUPPLY OF
ENLISTED
VOLUNTEERS

The Army is only one of many competitors for
the labor of the young men in the nation's manpower
pool, and its competitive position for this labor is
affected by the degree of national emergency, the unemployment rate of young male workers, the recruiting
efforts of the Army relative to those of other competitors, and the prevailing attitudes of society and
individuals toward the draft and military service.
The degree to which the Army may be compelled to rely
upon confiscatory policy instruments such as the Selective Service System for procurement of required
manpower may serve as a measure of its competitive
strength or weakness in a given market situation.

The experience of this country includes a broad
spectrum of military manpower procurement policies
ranging from nearly voluntary "employment," with little or no reliance upon a draft, to completely confiscatory procurement, such as occurred during most
of World War II. In the former situation, the Army
competes with civilian employers as well as with the
other military services; in the latter case, competition is virtually nonexistent and available manpower
is rationed among the military services and the critical civilian occupations.

The most likely market situations, however, fall
between these extremes and are characterized by low,
medium, or high "draft pressure," which may be defined
as the ratio of draft calls to total qualified, available manpower. A situation involving low draft pressure is the most competitive, since the services must
compete with civilian employers as well as with each

other. In periods of high draft pressure, competition is mainly interservice, since individuals who do not volunteer probably face involuntary induction, with attendant restrictions on freedom of choice and greater uncertainty with regard to training and assignment.

In this study, investigation is made of how effectively the Army can compete for the labor of the nation's youth if an all-volunteer system of military service is adopted.

CHARACTERISTICS OF DRAFT-MOTIVATED ENLISTEES

Uncertainty may easily be the most important psychological component of draft pressure. Philip M. Abelson, in a magazine editorial entitled "Student Anxiety," finds that "the focal source of discontent is the draft. Students dislike the prospect of an interruption in their lives just as they are contemplating graduate school, a career and marriage. Only part of the students will eventually be drafted. However, almost all live in tormenting uncertainty, unable to plan their lives. Few humans live comfortably for long periods under the stress of major uncertainty."[1] One may assume that Abelson's statement also applies to nonstudent groups subject to the draft. How great, then, is this pressure; what groups does it influence most heavily; and how may it trigger a decision to enlist rather than to be inducted?

Enlisted Men

A Department of Defense Survey of Active Duty Military Personnel in October, 1964, attempted to measure the extent of draft-motivated enlistments at that time and to relate this variable to selected characteristics of the enlistees polled. The results of this poll are presented in Table 8.

The following observations may be made from the tabulations in Table 8:

1. The Army had the highest proportion of draft-motivated enlistees (slightly greater than the Air Force).

2. The proportion of "pure" (that is, nondraft-motivated) volunteers was considerably greater in the younger age group (17-19-year-olds).

3. Draft-motivation increased substantially with increases in the educational level of the persons polled.

4. Mental Categories I and II combined contained a higher proportion of draft-motivated enlistees than either of the lower mental groups.

TABLE 8

Extent of Draft-Motivated Enlistments Among
Regular Enlisted Personnel on Their First
Tour of Active Duty, October, 1964
(by selected characteristics)

Characteristic	Percent Draft-Motivated
Service	
Army	43.2
Navy	32.6
Air Force	42.9
Marine Corps	30.4
Age at Enlistment	
17-19 years	31.4
20-25 years	57.9
Education	
Less than high school graduate	23.0
High school graduate	40.2
Some college or more	58.2
Mental Category	
Groups I and II	44.0
Group III	33.2
Group IV	29.2

Source: Reference Materials from the Department of Defense Study of the Draft, OASD (Manpower) (July, 1966), p. 18.6.

It should be noted that draft calls during the
period fiscal 1961-64, which was the period of entry
for almost all of the personnel polled, were far below the levels of the Korean War or the Vietnam
buildup. Draft calls during fiscal 1961 and 1963,
in fact, were the lowest during the entire period of
fiscal 1951-69. This period would appear to have
been a "seller's market" for the enlistees; therefore, the extent of draft-motivation is somewhat surprising.

At this point, a word of caution on the inter-
pretation of the percentages in Table 8 and subsequent tables is warranted. Historically, the numbers
and relative proportions of enlistees decrease as the
indices of age, education, mental category, and other
attributes reach higher values.

Age

Consider the age distribution of enlistees. In
fiscal 1967, more than 60 percent of Army enlistees
were age 19 or younger, and less than 40 percent were
age 20 or older. A weighted average of the percentages in Table 8 yields an overall percentage of draft-
motivated enlistments of 42 percent (.6[31.4 percent]
+ .4 [57.9 percent]). The implication to be drawn
from this is that the overall incidence of draft-
motivation is weighted toward the lower percentages
under each characteristic in the table.

The greater draft-motivation for the older age
group is not surprising, since this group has more
firmly established educational, career, and family
goals which may conflict with their military service
obligations. The recruiting goals of the U.S. Army
Recruiting Command (USAREC) and opinion surveys of
the general public reflect a common interest in military service entry at a relative young age. A public opinion survey conducted in October, 1963, posed
the following question: "If you had a son who had
to spend two years in the military service, at what
age would you like to have him begin the service?"
The response is reflected in Table 9. Of the 95 percent expressing opinions, 52.6 percent preferred age

18 or younger; 62.1 percent, age 19 or younger; 72.6 percent, age 20 or younger; and 90.5 percent, age 21 or younger.

TABLE 9

Age at Which General Public Prefers Young Men
To Enter Military Service

Age	Percent Preferring	Cumulative Percent
16	1	1
17	5	6
18	44	50
19	9	59
20	10	69
21	17	86
22	6	92
older	3	95
no opinion	5	100

Source: Unfit for Service (Chicago: Science Research Associates, Inc., September 1, 1966), p. 205.

According to a USAREC memorandum entitled "Recruiting Program Objectives for Fiscal Year 1968," study has established that 17-year-olds make up 15 percent of enlistees, while males aged 22 to 26 constitute less than 6 percent. This means that males aged 21 or younger constitute 94 percent of the Army's enlistees, which compares favorably with the preference of 90.5 percent of the general public for entry of young men into the military service before they reach the age of 22.

These findings are reconfirmed in the Ketchum, MacLeod & Grove, Inc., "Youth Attitude Trend Survey" for USAREC in May, 1967. This survey concludes that "the majority of youth entertain serious thoughts about military service while they are in high school (mainly in their junior and senior years) which reinforces the conclusion that communications efforts

should be concentrated against youth who are in the
process of completing their high school education."
It should be noted that age 18, which, according to
the survey summarized in Table 9, is most preferred
by the public as the age of entry into the military
service, is also the normal age for high school grad-
uation. The similarity of these findings from three
different sources indicates that USAREC is in step
with the national sentiment on the preferred age of
entry into military service.

Educational Level, Mental Category

The observations that draft-motivation increased
significantly with educational level and mental category can also be explained sociologically. Toward
the lower end of the educational/mental category spectrum are young men, largely high school dropouts and
marginal high school graduates, for whom military
service may represent a last chance to acquire the
training and skills needed for effective participation in today's society. Training programs, such as
Project 100,000 and Project Transition, which have
been instituted in the last few years, have undoubt-
edly increased the attractiveness of military service
to this group of men. Even young men rejected for
military service sometimes have recourse to programs
such as the Experimental and Demonstration Manpower
Project for Recruitment, Training, Placement, and
Followup of Army Rejectees conducted by the National
Committee for Children and Youth in conjunction with
the Department of Labor's Office of Manpower, Automa-
tion, and Training.

At the upper end of the educational/mental category spectrum is a group which exhibits a high degree
of draft motivation: 58 percent of the "some college
or more" category, and 44 percent of Mental Categories
I and II. The college-educated group is likely to be
older and more firmly committed to a nonmilitary future
than are the less educated groups. The higher mental
groups are more likely to be better educated (or, for
high school graduates, college-bound) than are the
lower groups.

Implications for Recruitment

The middle of the spectrum, which constitutes the major portion of today's enlisted manpower, probably consists largely of high school graduates without immediate plans for further civilian training or education. It is toward this group that USAREC directs most of its present communication and recruiting efforts. The wisdom of this allocation of recruiting resources appears to be borne out by the Ketchum, MacLeod & Grove survey, which concludes that "youth are most strongly interested and desirous of continuing their education and augmenting/improving their technical skills. Education/training responses are given most frequently as the benefit of military service, an important reason for choosing particular branches, and continues as a subject youth would like to know more about."

The findings and recommendations of the Ketchum, MacLeod & Grove 1967 survey are best summarized by the following extracts:

1. "Communications efforts should be concentrated against youth who are in the process of completing their high school education" for the following reasons:

   a. This is a time at which "most youth must and do consider alternatives for the future--education, career and employment, marriage, etc. Military service is one of these options."

   b. The sheer size of the market argues for strong consideration.

   c. Youth are more receptive to recruiting appeals at this stage because their career commitments are not yet definite.

2. "The expressed preference for enlistment as opposed to being drafted is ascribed primarily to negative attitudes toward the draft."

3. A "substantial minority" would prefer the
   draft because

   a. they would serve less time if drafted,
      and

   b. there is the possibility of avoiding
      military service altogether.

4. "The Army has shown significant improvement,
   and now ranks first, as the branch which
   does the best job of giving men information
   about itself. But there was no corresponding improvement in the Army's image."

5. "The perceived image of the Army continues
   to be most favorable, but overshadowed by
   the Air Force, in the following three areas:

   a. Largest choice of technical or vocational
      fields

   b. Technical training which will be most
      helpful in civilian life

   c. Best chance of getting the technical
      training desired."

First-Term Officers

A second poll taken during the Department of
Defense Survey of Active Duty Military Personnel in
October, 1964, provides data on the extent of draft-
motivated service among first-term officers. Table
10 presents the results of this poll.

The following may be noted from Table 10:

1. The Army has the highest proportion of draft-
   motivated first-term officers, approaching
   50 percent of the sample polled.

2. Predictably, the military academies, being
   rich in military tradition and maintaining
   high entrance standards, reflected the lowest incidence of draft-motivation.

3. OCS, ROTC, and officers entering the mili-
    tary service by direct appointments all re-
    flected about 50 percent draft-motivation.
    These percentages are reasonably close to
    those shown in Table 8 for enlisted men in
    the 20-to-25-year age group (57.9 percent),
    the "some college or more" educational group
    (58.0 percent), and Mental Categories I and
    II (44.0 percent). This similarity should
    not be surprising, since this age/education/
    mental category profile is generally charac-
    teristic of men qualified for commissions
    as officers. One can only surmise that these
    officers had some motivation in addition to
    that of their enlisted peers which led them
    to become officers--perhaps a desire to serve
    in a more prestigious position of leadership
    and the attraction of the higher pay and gen-
    erally better living conditions of officers.

TABLE 10

Extent of Draft-Motivated Service Among
First-Term Officers on Their First Tour
of Active Duty, October, 1964
(by selected characteristics)

Characteristic	Percent Draft-Motivated
Service	
Army	48.4
Navy	40.3
Air Force	38.9
Marine Corps	27.0
Source of Commission	
Academy	10.9
Officer Candidate School (OCS) or Officer Training School (OTS)	51.4
Reserve Officer Training Corps (ROTC)	45.4
Direct Appointment	57.8
Other	19.7

Source: Reference Materials from the Department
of Defense Study of the Draft, OASD (Manpower) (July,
1966), p. 18.7.

Reservists

The final table in this series reflects the incidence of draft-motivation among enlistees who entered a reserve component directly from civilian life.

TABLE 11

Extent of Draft-Motivation Among Enlistees
Who Entered the Reserve Components
Directly from Civilian Life
(by selected characteristics)

Characteristic	Percent Draft-Motivated
Component	
Army National Guard	68.3
Army Reserve	82.9
Navy Reserve	74.8
Marine Corps Reserve	49.9
Air National Guard	77.4
Air Force Reserve	86.5
Age at Enlistment	
17-19 years	39.6
20-21 years	77.1
22 and older	88.9
Education	
Less than high school graduate	31.0
High school graduate only	58.6
Some college (no degree)	71.1
College graduate or more	90.1
Annual Income	
Less than $2,999	54.1
$3,000-$4,999	71.6
$5,000-$7,499	72.1
$7,500 or more	82.2

Source: Reference Materials from the Department of Defense Study of the Draft, OASD (Manpower) (July, 1966), p. 18.8.

From Table 11 the following may be observed:

1. The extent of draft-motivation among en-
    listees in Army reserve components falls
    roughly in the middle range of the percent-
    age spectrum.

2. Increased draft-motivation with increasing
    age at the time of enlistment is much more
    pronounced among enlisted reservists than
    among regular enlisted personnel (see Table
    8). Presumably, a large proportion of the
    reservists aged 20 years and older had full-
    time civilian jobs when they enlisted and
    may have chosen a reserve component in order
    to minimize disruption of their career plans.

3. The extent of draft-motivation among enlist-
    ed reservists increases dramatically with
    educational attainment; the range between
    the groups with the lowest and those with
    the highest attainment (31.0 percent to 90.1
    percent) is much greater than it is in Table
    8 (23.0 percent to 58.2 percent). Again,
    there is probably a linkage with age and em-
    ployment status at the time of enlistment.

4. There is no significant difference in draft-
    motivation between enlisted reservists whose
    annual income is $3,000 to $4,999 and those
    whose annual income is $5,000 to $7,499. The
    lower percentage in the "less than $2,999"
    group is probably a function of the younger
    ages and lower educational levels in this
    group, just as the higher percentage in the
    "$7,500 or more" group is probably a function
    of older ages and higher educational levels.
    No comparison with Table 8 in this respect
    is possible.

In summary, the information in Table 11 might
provide ammunition to contemporary critics who allege
that the reserve components are a haven for draft-
dodgers. In cases where comparison with Table 8 is
possible, draft-motivation among enlisted reservists

is higher than draft-motivation among their peers on
active duty. Reservists predictably reflect a strong-
er motivation to minimize their active duty tours
than do regular enlisted first-termers.

Summary

No attempt has been made to attach connotations
of "good" or "bad" to the low or high incidence of
draft-motivation for each category in Tables 8, 10,
and 11. From the Army's point of view, it is desirable to obtain maximum performance from each individual soldier, and there is no evidence of any differential in the performance of "pure" volunteers and
draft-induced volunteers. Tables 8, 10, and 11 show
that the draft-motivation is highest among men who are
older, better educated, and in higher mental categories, and that the draft induces many of this group
to seek commissions through ROTC and OCS programs.

IMAGE OF THE ARMY

The image of the Army is certainly an element in
the Army's success or failure in competing with other
services for qualified manpower. Under a draft system, a young man who is negatively inclined toward
military service, but favorably impressed by the Army,
may be triggered into Army enlistment when the burden
of uncertainty created by the pressure of the draft
becomes sufficiently great. Under an all-volunteer
system, the image of the Army will almost certainly
be a critical factor. The results of a survey conducted for the Army by Opinion Research Corporation
in the spring of 1969 are helpful in understanding
the image of the Army currently held by the public.[2]

The most significant finding of this survey is
that less than half (41 percent) of the Vietnam veterans interviewed described their overall impressions
of the Army as "very favorable" or "mostly favorable."
This contrasts sharply with nearly two-thirds (65 percent) of World War II and Korea veterans who described
their impressions as favorable. Furthermore, close

to one-quarter (22 percent) of the Vietnam veterans
said they had "mostly unfavorable" or "very unfavorable"
impressions of the Army. The greatest dissatisfac-
tion existed among men who served two years and among
nonwhites. Less than 10 percent of World War II and
Korea veterans had such unfavorable impressions.

An equally significant finding is that Vietnam
veterans going to college at the time of the survey
had the least favorable impression of Army life.
Nearly three in ten (29 percent) had "mostly unfavorable" or "very unfavorable" impressions, and not one
pleaded "no opinion." Vietnam veterans in college
(70 percent) also felt that most other students on
their campuses had basically unfavorable attitudes
toward the Army. However, 58 percent of them thought
that Army service would make college students more
favorably inclined toward the Army. The special cir-
cumstance of the war in Vietnam may be a major con-
tributing factor in creating the current climate of
veteran opinion.

On the other hand, many veterans included G.I.
education benefits among the benefits they gained
from military service. More than 60 percent of Vietnam veterans (92 percent of those in college) mentioned educational benefits. Since college looms
large in readjustment to civilian life, educational
benefits are certainly a significant incentive. However, these benefits could be extended widely to include not only colleges, universities, and junior
colleges but also trade schools and vocational schools,
so that more ex-servicemen could be assisted in achiev-
ing a satisfying civilian career. The Reemployment
Service of the U.S. Department of Labor reports that
there are approximately one million ex-servicemen re-
turning to civilian life each year. Of these, only
about two-thirds had jobs when they entered the armed
forces and only 40 percent had sufficient employment
and appropriate length of service to enable them to
apply to the Reemployment Service for assistance.
This means that more than half a million ex-servicemen
have to achieve a civilian career without the benefit
of the Reemployment Service.

The U.S. Training and Employment Service (operating through the state employment services) has a Veterans Placement Service staff which works in the states on behalf of all veterans, including those without jobs prior to military service. However, it is not clear how much counseling and guidance is provided, and some of these veterans may require intensive counseling and guidance. It is understood that a study is being conducted on a sample of ex-servicemen who have returned to civilian life in order to determine their adjustment. Such a study is urgently needed.

In conclusion, the establishment of an image is both an inside and an outside job. Advertising, salesmanship, publicity, and all the other techniques of image-creation are valuable and essential. But the readjustments on the inside are even more important. It is the package of reforms which the Army installs that will be the crucial factor in creating a sound and solid image which will produce volunteers who stay with the organization and recommend it to others when they leave.

ESTIMATES OF THE SUPPLY OF ENLISTED VOLUNTEERS

The factors which may motivate a man to enlist in the Army are many and complicated. Voluntary enlistment may be motivated by a desire to reduce individual uncertainty created by the possibility of being drafted, by patriotic or duty-oriented beliefs, by family tradition, by career-oriented employment goals, or by any combination of these and other attitudinal variables. Each of the possible motives for enlistment will vary in importance to an individual according to the likelihood of his being drafted, the appeal to him of the work which the Army happens to be performing, the relative strength to him of the Army's "sales pitch," and myriad other environmental factors. The problems involved in obtaining a "surprise-free" prediction of the response of young men en masse to a set of circumstance-dependent stimuli cannot be over-stressed. Furthermore, the qualitative aspects of the future environments for Army

manpower procurement may be perceived only in general
terms, and even present and past youth attitudes are
largely unarticulated.

Given the Army's requirement for manpower, the
problem is to estimate the number of men who will enlist under an all-volunteer system of military service.

Description of Equation Used

Acknowledging the complexity of interaction
among the attitudinal factors which may motivate enlistment, the primary concern in this chapter is measuring the supply response of potential volunteers to
changes in economic conditions. More specifically,
an attempt is made to measure response to changes in
military compensation, which is the only economic
variable subject to policy control by the military.
Since enlistments are also affected by changes in conditions in the civilian economy (described by measures
of income and unemployment), a supply equation for
volunteers can be written as

$$(1) \quad \frac{E}{P} = \alpha + \beta_1 \ln\left(\frac{W_c}{W_m}\right) + \beta_2 \ln(1-U) + \beta_3 \ln\left(1 - \frac{A}{P}\right) + \mu$$

where E = enlistments (Mental Categories I-III),*
P = population, W_c = civilian income, W_m = military
compensation, U = the unemployment rate, A = accessions (enlistments plus inductions), and μ represents
random variation.

Equation (1) represents the enlistment rate $\left(\frac{E}{P}\right)$
as a function of the natural logarithms of relative
pay (i.e., the ratio of civilian pay to military pay),
of the unemployment rate in the civilian economy,

---

*Accessions from the upper portion of Mental
Category IV were omitted because enlistments from
this mental category are limited in peacetime by
recruitment quotas. See Appendix B.

and of the accession rate $\left(\frac{A}{P}\right)$ into the military.
Since the decision to enlist is not free, i.e., since
enlistment rates are affected by the presence of a
draft as well as by the economic conditions mentioned
above, the accession rate is written into the equation to represent the effect of manpower procurement
by the military on enlistment response. The form of
Equation (1) is derived from the theoretical argu-
ments in Fisher's paper.[3]

An important property of this equation is that
the elasticity of enlistment response to a change in
military pay is a decreasing function of the enlistment rate. That is, the lower the enlistment rate,
the higher the elasticity of response to a change in
pay; the higher the enlistment rate, the lower the
elasticity of response. What this says is that, in
attracting additional volunteers through increases
in pay or other compensation, it becomes increasingly difficult (that is, more expensive) to attract a
given percentage increment.

The parameters of Equation (1) have been estimated using both time-series and cross-section data,
both for the Army and for the Department of Defense
as a whole. (See Appendix B for a description of
this data.) The results of the estimation have been
used to suggest the magnitude of the increase in military compensation necessary to attract sufficient
numbers of volunteers to maintain a force of 2.65 million men in all the services combined. This is pre-
sumably the size of a force adequate for "peacekeeping"
purposes.

Estimation with Time-Series Data

Using time-series data (third quarter, 1958,
through fourth quarter, 1965), estimates are made for
all DOD as

$$(2) \quad \frac{E_2}{P_2} = .0031 - \underset{(.0096)}{.0224} \ln \left(\frac{W_c}{W_{m2}}\right) - \underset{(.0214)}{.0256} \ln (1-U_3)$$

$$- \underset{(.1043)}{.4167} \ln \left(1 - \frac{A_2}{P_2}\right) \qquad R^2 = .64$$

and for the Army as

$$(3) \quad \frac{E_1}{P_2} = .0010 - \underset{(.0026)}{.0089} \ln\left(\frac{W_c}{W_{m1}}\right) - \underset{(.0067)}{.0132} \ln (1-U_3)$$

$$- \underset{(.0426)}{.1350} \ln \left(1 - \frac{A_1}{P_2}\right)$$

$$+ \underset{(.0004)}{.00051D_1} - \underset{(.0004)}{.0001D_2}$$

$$+ \underset{(.0004)}{.0012D_3} \qquad\qquad R^2 = .77$$

where E_1 = Army enlistments (Mental Categories I-III),
E_2 = all DOD enlistments (Mental Categories I-III),
W_c = median civilian earnings, W_{m1} = average compensation in the Army, W_{m2} = average compensation in all
the services combined, P_2 = available population,
U_3 = the unemployment rate for civilian males aged
18-19, A_1 = total Army accessions, A_2 = total DOD
accessions, and D_1, D_2, D_3 = seasonal dummy variables.
(See Appendix B for precise definitions of these variables, for a listing of sources, and for a description of data manipulation.) The figures in parentheses are standard errors of the estimated coefficients.

Elasticities of enlistment response to changes
in relative pay are calculated from the formula which
is derived from Equation (1)

$$(4) \qquad\qquad\qquad \epsilon = \frac{b_1}{\dfrac{E}{P}}$$

where b_1 = the estimate of the pay coefficient β_1
and $\frac{E}{P}$ = the enlistment rate. These elasticities
(around the mean enlistment rate without a draft) are
-2.78 and -2.40 for all DOD and the Army, respectively. That is, a 1 percent change in relative pay would
be expected to elicit a change of 2.78 percent in the
enlistment rate for the entire DOD and 2.4 percent in
the rate for the Army.

Estimation with Cross-Section Data

Estimates of the parameters of Equation (1) were also made using cross-section data taken from Altman's article.[4]   (It should be noted that these data have only nine observations.) However, the variable measuring accessions $\left(\ln \left[1 - \frac{A}{P}\right]\right)$ is dropped from Equation (1) under the assumption that draft pressure is felt uniformly across the country. In this case, the estimate made for the Department of Defense is

$$(5) \quad \frac{E}{P} = .1202 - \underset{(.0298)}{.0978} \ln \left(\frac{W_c}{W_m}\right)$$

$$- \underset{(.1537)}{.2262} \ln (1-U) \qquad R^2 = .67$$

and that for the Army is

$$(6) \quad \frac{E}{P} = .0376 - \underset{(.0098)}{.0421} \ln \left(\frac{W_c}{W_m}\right)$$

$$- \underset{(.0509)}{.0853} \ln (1-U) \qquad R^2 = .77$$

Elasticities of enlistment response to changes in relative pay are calculated at the mean enlistment rate without a draft as -.82 and -1.19 for all DOD and the Army, respectively. That is, a 1 percent change in relative pay would be expected to elicit a change of slightly less than 1 percent in the enlistment rate for the Department of Defense and slightly more than 1 percent in the rate for the Army. Again, the form of the estimating equation requires that all elasticities decrease as the enlistment rate is increased.

Calculation of Required Compensation

On the basis of the estimates made in Equations (2), (3), (5), and (6), and projected values for civilian income (W_C), unemployment (U), and population (P), the level of military compensation (W_m) required to attract any desired number of volunteers can be easily calculated.

Restating Equation (1) in a different form, the following equation is obtained:*

$$(7) \quad \frac{E}{P} = \frac{\alpha}{1+\beta_3} + \frac{\beta_1}{1+\beta_3} \ln \left(\frac{W_C}{W_m} \right)$$

$$+ \frac{\beta_2}{1+\beta_3} \ln (1-U) - \frac{\beta_3}{1+\beta_3} \left(\frac{I}{P} \right)$$

where I = inductions.

---

*From Equation (1)

$$\frac{E}{P} = \alpha + \beta_1 \ln \left(\frac{W_C}{W_m} \right) + \beta_2 \ln (1-U) + \beta_3 \ln \left(1 - \frac{A}{P} \right),$$

the following transformation is made:

$$\frac{E}{P} = \alpha + \beta_1 \ln \left(\frac{W_C}{W_m} \right) + \beta_2 \ln (1-U) - \beta_3 \left(\frac{A}{P} \right)$$

since $\ln \left(1 - \frac{A}{P} \right) \simeq - \frac{A}{P}$ for $\left| \frac{A}{P} \right|$ close to zero; and

$$\frac{E}{P} = \alpha + \beta_1 \ln \left(\frac{W_C}{W_m} \right) + \beta_2 \ln (1-U) - \beta_3 \left(\frac{E}{P} + \frac{I}{P} \right)$$

where I = inductions. From the above equation, Equation (1) can be written as

$$\frac{E}{P} = \frac{\alpha}{1+\beta_3} + \frac{\beta_1}{1+\beta_3} \ln \left(\frac{W_C}{W_m} \right) + \frac{\beta_2}{1+\beta_3} \ln (1-U) - \frac{\beta_3}{1+\beta_3} \left(\frac{I}{P} \right)$$

Substituting into Equation (7) the estimated
values for α, β_1, β_2, and β_3 from Equation (2), along
with projected values for P, W_c and U, and setting
I = 0 (i.e., no inductions), the increase in annual
military compensation (W_m) required to attract
644,000 volunteers into the Department of Defense
each year is calculated as $254 per man. For the
Army, using the estimated values for the parameters
of Equation (3), along with the same projected values
for the independent variables (P, W_c, U, and I), the
increase in W_m required to attract 322,000 volunteers
annually* is calculated as $1,370 per man. For both
DOD and the Army, these calculations are based on the
assumptions that P = 11 million, U = .15, and W_c =
$3,600 per year.

Implications of the Calculations

The results of the calculations above have a
number of implications. If we assume that 83 percent
of the Army's enlisted strength of 858,615 men are
first-termers** and the other 17 percent are careerists,
the annual wage bill for first-termers would be $3.515
billion (712,650 x $4,932) at the new rate of compen-
sation, and the wage bill for this force at the current rate would be $2.538 billion (712,650 x $3,562).
Assuming that the $1,370 pay increase would also go
to careerists, the annual wage bill for them at the
new rate would be $1.197 billion (145,965 x $8,200).
At the present rate, the careerists' annual wage bill
would be $0.997 billion (145,965 x $6,830).*** This

----

*The assumption is made that the Army will re-
quire 322,000 accessions each year to maintain a
"peacekeeping" force and that DOD will require twice
this number. This assumption will be challenged later.

**Based on the inventory of enlisted men projected
for 1975 by the inventory model (for a hypothetical
"peacekeeping" force).

***The wage figures used to determine wage bill
at current rate are weighted average wages at present
rates of compensation, as calculated by the inventory
model.

means the overall Army wage bill at the increased rate
of compensation derived from the equations would be
$1.2 billion per year higher than that calculated at
the current rate. It is apparent that the pay increase for a first-termer would be about 38 percent.

Similar calculations can be made for the Department of Defense as a whole on the basis of Equation
(2). In this study, however, the supply equation for
DOD has been disregarded and all cost estimates have
been based on Equation (3) for the Army. Since the
Army is the only service which depends on the draft
for a major portion of its manpower, the wage established under an all-volunteer system must be high
enough to attract men into the Army, or it will fail
in its purpose. Furthermore, as discussed below, in
the absence of a draft, the elasticity of the enlistment rate with respect to pay is lower for the Army
than for DOD as a whole.

In an all-volunteer system all accessions are
by definition enlistments (i.e., E = A), and the form
of Equation (1) implies that the pay increase necessary to attract a sufficient number of volunteers
varies as the number of required accessions (E) varies
(as a result of changes in the force level) and as the
size of the available male population (P) expands.

This is true because the required accession rate
$\left(\frac{E}{P}\right)$ depends on both E and P. If the number of annual
accessions (E) is constant and the population (P)
steadily increases, the required enlistment rate will
decrease and the military compensation necessary to
attract that number of accessions will also decrease.
The same would be true if accessions steadily de-
creased.

Figures 2 and 3 illustrate the effects on military compensation of changes in population and in
accessions required for the Army. The vertical axis
in both graphs shows the required (or minimum) ratio
of military compensation (W_{m1}) to civilian earnings
(W_c). The horizontal axis in Figure 2 shows the number of accessions required (E_1) if the available population is 11 million. The horizontal axis in Figure
3 shows the number of available civilian males (P_2);

FIGURE 2

The Relationship Between Required Army Enlistment
and Military Compensation Relative to Civilian Income
(for an available population of 11 million)

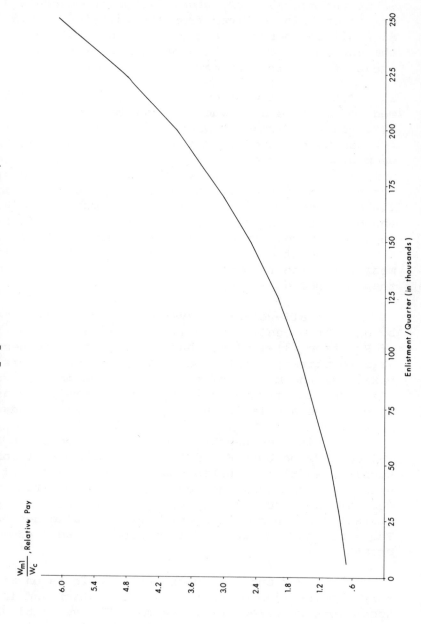

FIGURE 3

The Relationship Between Available Civilian Male Population
and Military Compensation Relative to Civilian Income
(for annual accession of 322,000)

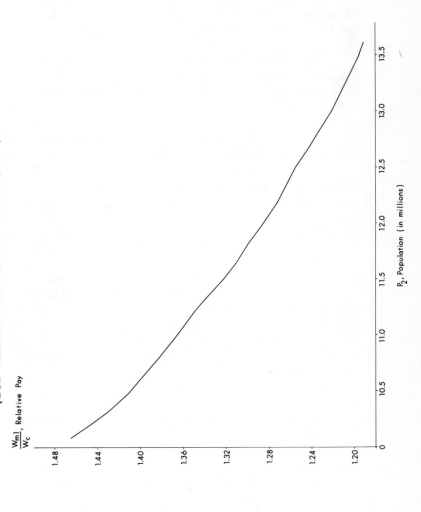

this graph is based on the assumption that Army accessions remain constant at 322,000 each year. Equation (3) was used in developing both these graphs
under the assumptions that there are no inductions
($I = 0$) and the unemployment rate (U_3) for males aged
18-19 years is 0.15. The definitions of the variables
used are found in Appendix B.

The major conclusion for this section is that as
the size of the force increases, it is increasingly
difficult to attract the necessary number of volunteers simply by increasing compensation.

From a purely economic point of view, as the
force grows beyond a certain size, it will be less
expensive to offer incentives than to offer higher
and higher pay. From a practical point of view, any
force larger than the force level deemed sufficient
for "peacekeeping" implies the existence of limited
or major conflict and, hence, eventual reduction of
the force to a preconflict level. This eventual
necessity for reduction suggests that, in building the
force, incentives should be adopted which will function as counterincentives after the conflict. Such
counterincentives will be necessary to force down the
higher retention rates which are probable if a high
level of military compensation is instituted prior
to the conflict, maintained through the conflict, and
continued after it. The G.I. Bill is an outstanding
example of such an incentive; it serves well to attract volunteers during a period of conflict and yet
returns a large proportion of servicemen to civilian
life after the conflict. Furthermore, fluctuation in
military compensation would be potentially a most de-
moralizing factor. All these points argue for a combination of pay and incentives when the size of the
force grows past a certain point.

COMPARISON OF RESULTS WITH EARLIER STUDIES

In order to discuss the implications of the results described in the preceding section, comparisons
with earlier studies are made.*

----

*In October, 1969, when the results of this study

Fisher has made an estimate of enlistment response based on the form of Equation (1), using quarterly time-series data (third quarter, 1957, through fourth quarter, 1965).[5] The major difference between Fisher's data and the data used in estimating enlistment response in this study is the definition of available population.* Fisher's estimation of the enlistment rate for the entire Department of Defense is

$$(8) \quad \frac{E}{P} = .0075 - \underset{(.00324)}{.00709} \ln \left(\frac{W_c}{W_m}\right) - \underset{(.01018)}{.00891} \ln (1-U)$$

$$- \underset{(.041)}{.3120} \ln \left(1 - \frac{A}{P}\right)$$

$$- \underset{(.00069)}{.00133SP} + \underset{(.00065)}{.00254SU}$$

$$- \underset{(.00056)}{.00196A} \qquad\qquad R^2 = .90$$

in which $\ln \left(\frac{W_c}{W_m}\right)$ and $\ln (1-U)$ were lagged one quarter.

---

were submitted to the Army, the President's Commission on an All-Volunteer Armed Force had not yet concluded its study. The Commission's report was published in February, 1970, but its working papers were still unavailable to the public when this study was being prepared for publication. Since the published report of the Commission did not include a detailed description of methodology, it was decided not to analyze the Commission's results in this volume.

*In this study (Equations (2) and (3)), P_2 is defined as the average number of Selective Service registrants in the 50 states and the District of Columbia over a specified calendar quarter--excluding 1A and 1AO registrants aged 26 and over and all registrants whose classification status was 1Y, 4F, 1C, 4A, or 5A. Fisher's population consists of male civilians aged 17-20.

The variables are defined as they were for
Equation (1), except that SP, SU, and A are seasonal
dummy variables for spring, summer, and autumn, respectively.

Altman's estimates of enlistment response are
based on constant elasticity supply equations and
1963 cross-section data.[6] (These same data were used
by the authors of this study for Equations (5) and
(6) described in the previous section.) Altman's estimates of supply for DOD and the Army, respectively,
are

(9) $\ln \frac{E}{P} = -1.8287 + .80332 \ln \left(\frac{W_m}{W_c}\right)$
                      $(.2625)$

              $+ .34348 \ln U \qquad R^2 = .69$
              $(.1598)$

(10) $\ln \frac{E}{P} = -4.5051 + 1.0399 \ln \left(\frac{W_m}{W_c}\right)$
                       $(.3050)$

              $+ .41167 \ln U \qquad R^2 = .74$
              $(.1863)$

The tables below summarize the elasticities of
enlistment response to change in the ratio of military
pay to civilian pay estimated by Equations (2), (3),
(5), (6), (8), (9), and (10). The elasticities estimated by all equations but Altman's (which assume
constant elasticity) are calculated at the mean enlistment rate.

These tables show that Equations (2) and (3),
which are used in this study, are most elastic.
Notice that, according to these equations, the elasticity of the enlistment rate is lower for DOD than
for the Army with the draft and higher for DOD than
the Army without the draft. This contrasts markedly
with the results of other equations and indicates
that the enlistment rate for DOD as a whole is more
influenced by draft pressure than is the enlistment
rate for the Army. With elimination of the draft,
therefore, the elasticity of enlistment response to

change in the ratio of military pay to civilian pay will be higher for DOD than for the Army. It is for this reason that estimates of the cost of a volunteer force in this study are based on the elasticity of enlistment response for the Army. (See the section immediately below for additional comment on the effect of the draft on enlistments.)

TABLE 12

Mean Elasticity of Enlistment in DOD
with Respect to Compensation

Equation	With draft	Without draft
Fisher (8)	.46	.74
Altman (9)	.38	.80
Kim-Farrell- Fisher (2)	1.73	2.78
Fisher-Kim (5)	.12	.82

TABLE 13

Mean Elasticity of Enlistment in Army
with Respect to Compensation

Equation	With draft	Without draft
Altman (10)	.54	1.10
Kim-Farrell Fisher (3)	1.94	2.40
Fisher-Kim (6)	.46	1.19

The study made by Walter Oi and the study made jointly by Altman and Alan Fechter[7] are not evaluated here because the assumptions on which they base their

cost estimates for an all-volunteer force of 2.65
million men are not clear to the authors of this
study. Oi's estimate of additional cost is $4 bil-
lion per year; Altman-Fechter's estimate of additional cost is between $5.4 and $8.3 billion per year.
Their estimates of the annual accessions necessary
to maintain a force of 2.65 million are much lower
than the estimate of accessions in this study. If
the estimate of accessions used in this study were
to be used by Oi and Altman-Fechter in developing
cost estimates based on their equations, the cost of
an all-volunteer force would be prohibitively high.

Judging from the elasticity of the supply equations estimated for this study, the cost of raising
military pay enough to attract any given number of
enlistments will be lower than that estimated by the
other studies. The table below illustrates the point.
It compares the ratio of military pay to civilian
earnings estimated by this study to be necessary to
induce 644,000 men each year to enlist in all the
services combined without the draft to the ratios
estimated to be necessary by the other studies.
(Since eligible population (P) is defined differently
for each equation, the equivalent (P) for each equation was calculated for this comparison. Fisher's
population, male civilians aged 17-20, can be easily
derived from the civilian manpower pool model including 4Fs and 1Ys developed for this study. For
Altman's population, see Table 7.)

IMPLICATIONS OF RESULTS

Effect of the Draft on Enlistments

According to an attitude survey conducted by the
Department of Defense in 1964,[8] approximately 38 percent of all volunteers and 43 percent of volunteers
to the Army are draft-motivated. A more recent sample survey of Army enlistees (April, 1969) indicates
that 49.7 percent are draft-motivated. The higher
percentage of reluctant volunteers to the Army in
recent years may be a result of the war in Southeast
Asia.

TABLE 14

Comparison of Ratio of Military Pay to Civilian
Earnings Necessary to Maintain "Peacekeeping"
Force, as Determined in This and
Other Studies

Equations for DOD	Assumptions	Ratio of military pay to civilian earnings
Fisher (8)	P = 8 million U = .15	2
Altman (9)	P = 1.2 million U = .15	10
Kim-Farrell- Fisher (2)	P = 11 million U = .15	1.06
Fisher-Kim (5)	P = 1.2 million U = .15	48.5

Source: Calculated from results of equations.

Using Equations (2) and (3), the estimated mean
enlistment rates $\left(\frac{E}{P}\right)$ with and without the draft are
calculated for DOD and the Army. The rate for DOD is
.01297 with the draft and .00804 without the draft,
the draft-motivated rate is .00493, and the percent
draft-motivated (.00493/.01297) is 38 percent. The
rate for the Army is .00459 with the draft and .00371
without the draft, the draft-motivated rate is .00088,
and the percent draft-motivated is 20 percent.

It is evident that the percentage of draft-
motivated enlistees in all the services calculated
from Equation (2) (38 percent) is identical with the
results of the 1964 DOD survey. This may be entirely
coincidental. The difference between the degree of
draft-motivation calculated from the Equation (3) for

Army enlistees (20 percent) and the degree of draft-
motivation reported by the 1969 Army survey (49.7
percent) may be due to an overestimate by the survey
of the effect of the draft on enlistments. (Inciden-
tally, the survey was taken at induction centers.)
It may also result from the fact that the regression
analysis from which Equations (2) and (3) were derived covers the entire period from late 1958 through
1965, while the survey was taken at a single point in
time in 1969. It is possible, in fact, that the proportion of genuine volunteers in the Army is about
the same as the overall proportion of genuine volunteers in all the other services combined.[9] Certainly,
the Army's 1969 survey indicates this is the case.
In this survey, approximately 89 percent of the young
men who said they would have enlisted in the Army
whether or not there was a draft reported that they
had not even tried to enlist in another service. Ap-
parently, men who enlist in the Army genuinely prefer
the Army--for whatever reason. (It is conceivable
that one of the major reasons for preferring enlistment in the Army to enlistment in one of the other
services is that the enlistment period in the Army is
shorter--usually three years rather than four.)

Still another possible source for the difference between the percentage of draft-motivated calculated from Equation (3) and the percentage reported
in the 1969 survey is that any prediction from a
regression analysis is associated with increasing errors as the difference between the projected value of
the explanatory variable and its mean increases. Thus,
the coefficient of draft pressure may reliably predict
the effect on the enlistment rate of small changes
around the mean induction rate, but not of a change
of 100 percent (i.e., of a drop to zero) in the rate.

Effect of Unemployment on Enlistments

Statistics of unemployment in the more distant
past were significant for Army recruiters insofar as
they pictured reasonably well the general state of the
job market in the civilian economy. When unemployment
was high, the unemployed had a strong incentive to enlist in the Army. However, for the last quarter of a
century, there has been no major economic depression

and the overall rate of unemployment has not been a
significant factor in Army enlistment.

In any case, the overall rate of unemployment
in today's economy is not a good indicator of enlistment potential because it reflects many factors that
have little bearing on the job prospects of young men
of military age. The overall rate includes unemployed
adult men 20 years of age and over, adult women 20
years of age and over, and boys and girls 16-19 years
of age. The unemployment rate which should be much
more significant for enlistment incentives is the
rate for young men 16-24 years of age--particularly
the rate for 18- and 19-year-olds, the group from
which about 85 percent of enlistees are drawn. A
comparison of unemployment rates with enlistments in
recent years (see Figure 4) shows that fluctuations
in overall employment have had little influence upon
enlistments. The overall rate is significant only
insofar as it pictures the general condition of the
economy as a whole.

Clearly, the unemployment rate of young men 18-
19 years of age is much more significant. But comparison shows that fluctuations in this rate are less
significant than fluctuations in draft pressure.
While unemployment rates have been declining in the
last few years, the draft pressure created by the war
in Vietnam has caused enlistments to increase.

In general, unemployment rates for nonwhites are
about twice as high as the rates for whites. For
nonwhite males 18-19 years of age, the average unemployment rate in 1964 (prior to the buildup in Vietnam) was about 23 percent; during this period, nonwhite enlistments in the Army averaged about 3,300
a quarter. In 1967-68, when the unemployment rate for
nonwhite males 18-19 years of age averaged less than
20 percent, nonwhite enlistments averaged 5,000 to
5,500 per quarter. The impact of the draft has overshadowed any influence that unemployment might have
on the tendency of young men to enlist in the Army.

In assessing these facts, it is necessary to
look at some long-run trends in population and employment which have been obscured by developments in

FIGURE 4

Enlistments (Mental Categories I-III) and Inductions into the Army, 1958-69
(in relation to unemployment)

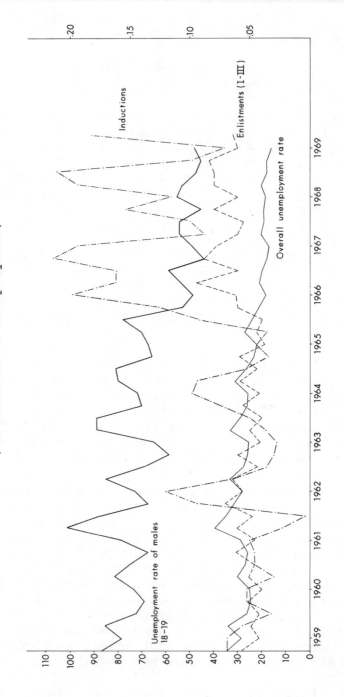

Vietnam. One trend is the marked increase in the
number of young men of military age and of working
age. If it had not been for the expansion of the
armed forces beginning in 1965, the number of young
men seeking work (and their unemployment rates) would
surely have been higher than they have been. Furthermore, the release of men from the armed forces during
the next few years will surely affect the unemployment rates of young workers trying to enter the labor
market. Stating the matter bluntly, the unemployment
of young men (and young women, too) is likely to be
substantially higher in the early 1970's than in the
late 1960's.[10]

However, there are two important factors which
will tend to dampen the impact of increased unemployment among youth on enlistment in the future. One of
them is that high unemployment rates are due in part
to the educational explosion which is taking such a
high proportion of young men into high school and
college. Many of these young men alternate between
work in the summer months and school in the winter,
or hold part-time jobs while attending school. This
means they enter and leave the labor force frequently,
with the likelihood of unemployment during entry
(before finding a job) or after leaving(before entering
school). From an analysis of the unemployment statistics we estimate that high school and college atten-
dance, combined with periodic jobseeking and employment, exerts a significant influence on the unemployment rates of young men up to at least 24 years of age.

The meaningful point about these figures is that
most of these young men are not in dire economic
straits. Their participation in the labor force has
a high degree of fluidity--from school to work, from
one job to another, from work back to school. The
great majority of them are by no means "down and out."

The second factor, which will further dampen any
connection between unemployment and enlistment, is the
expansion of government training and work programs
for young people, particularly the disadvantaged.
Among these are the Neighborhood Youth Corps, College
Work Study, the Jobs-in-Industry program--all of which

put young people to work. There are also the Job
Corps, the College Studies Program, and Manpower Development and Training Act programs which take young
people out of the job market for a time by supporting
them in training and education. Thus, any economic
incentive to enlist that might arise from youthful
unemployment is almost certain to be partly offset
by these programs. Furthermore, there is evidence
of intent on the part of the government to expand
these programs until practically all eligible young-
sters are covered, if they wish to be.

A high proportion of the young men in these
training and work programs are nonwhite, and this is
likely to continue in the future. Not only are unemployment and poverty much more serious among the
nonwhite population, but the proportion of nonwhites
among men in younger age groups is increasing. Statistics show that about 10 percent of the male population 25 years of age and over is nonwhite. The
ratio of nonwhites to whites in the group aged 20-24
is about one to eight; in the group aged 16-19 it is
nearly 1 to 7. Thus, during the 1970's, the proportion of nonwhites of military age will be higher than
it has been in recent decades.

The point of this analysis, however, is that
while young men may have a harder time breaking into
the civilian labor market in the future, they will
have the benefit of remedial programs designed to
keep them from unemployment and poverty. Therefore,
if the Army is to compete successfully with civilian
"employers," it will have to induce these employed
or employable young men to choose an Army career for
economic reasons.

The pay in government remedial programs will be
at the level of the minimum wage, or somewhat lower.
For example, in the work-training programs of the
early 1960's, young people were paid the minimum hourly wage for six hours each day and were required to
take two hours of training without pay. The result
was that the daily wage of these young trainees was
below the earnings of a person working at the hourly
minimum.

Assuming an Army pay scale that is competitive with the minimum wage of comparable full-time earners, there will still be plenty of economic incentive for these young men to enlist--not because they are unemployed but because the pay and prospects in the Army would be better. On a 52-week, 40-hours-a-week job the present federal minimum wage of $1.60 an hour would provide full-year earnings of $3,328. The size of the military pay differential will be the key to the possibility of attracting some of these young men into military service.

In conclusion, although Equations (2) and (3) imply that the unemployment rate of male civilians aged 18-19 has a statistically significant influence upon Army enlistments, the use of this unemployment rate as an explanatory variable has only limited significance for Army manpower planners. Since neither the Army nor DOD has any control over unemployment, its influence on the enlistment rate is wholly fortuitous. Unless the civilian economy experiences another major depression of the magnitude of the 1930's (with an overall unemployment rate of 25 per cent), DOD will have to assume that unemployment will be a minor factor in inducing enlistment in a volunteer Army.

Impact of Reenlistment Rates on Cost of a Volunteer Army

If total DOD strength were 2.65 million, the Army's enlisted strength would be approximately 858,000. At this force level, the total number of accessions required by the Army each year would actually be less under an all-volunteer system than the 322,000 annually projected by this study's inventory model for enlisted men. The assumption made in the model was that current rates of loss and retention will continue into the future. However, higher military pay and better-motivated enlistees under an all-volunteer system are expected to result in higher retention rates. Oi has estimated that accessions in an all-volunteer system need be only 70 per cent of accessions in a draft system.[11] If his estimate is correct, the Army will need only 225,000 accessions

annually. This implies that the wage bill necessary
to sustain a force of 858,000 under an all-volunteer
system would be much less than indicated earlier in
this chapter.

Incentives Versus Pay

According to the 1969 sample survey of Army enlistees cited earlier in this chapter, the incentives
(other than pay) which would be most attractive to
enlistees are "paid higher education" and "guarantee
of choice of job" after termination of service. Assuming that one-third of the young men enlisting in
the Army each year receive a four-year college education (at an annual cost of $2,000) and that another
third receive two years of training in a vocational
school (at an annual cost of $1,500),* the total an-
nual cost of these incentives to the Army would be
$1.2 billion.**

Another incentive mentioned in the Army survey
was an entry bonus of $2,000. If every enlistee were
paid $2,000, the total cost to the Army would be $644
million ($2,000 x 322,000). From the point of view
of sustaining a higher retention rate, it is greatly
preferable to offer an entry bonus than to offer education after service. The offer of either higher
education or guarantee of job will act as a counter-
incentive to retention. In addition, it is obviously
cheaper to offer an entry bonus than to offer higher
education ($644 million for bonuses rather than $1.2
billion for higher education). Furthermore, as discussed earlier in this chapter, increasing basic pay
and allowances for enlisted men enough to attract

----

*These cost figures are taken from a study by the
Department of Health, Education and Welfare which projected to 1979 the average charges in institutions of
higher education for full-time, degree-credit, resident, undergraduate students (in 1968-69 dollars).

**1/3 (322,000) x $8,000 + 1/3 (322,000) x
$3,000 = $1.181 billion.

322,000 volunteers each year under an all-volunteer
system will increase the cost of pay to the Army at
least $1.2 billion over current cost. This is the
same amount it would cost to offer higher education
as an incentive, but it is probable that higher pay
would result in a permanently higher retention rate,
while offering higher education (or choice of job in
postservice civilian life) would have an adverse effect on the retention rate.

The major question still remains: Under an all-
volunteer system, would the Army be able to compete
effectively with the other services for volunteers
if all the services offered the same pay? The estimated elasticity of enlistment response for the Army
to change in relative pay is lower than the estimated
elasticity of enlistment response for DOD in the absence of the draft. (See Equations (2) and (3).)
This suggests that under an all-volunteer system the
Army may have to pay a differential over the other
services or improve its image to potential enlistees.

In conclusion, it must be emphasized that detailed
studies should be made to determine the most advantag-
eous combination of pay and incentives. Any recommendations made as a result of such studies (and whatever
programs may be based on them) should be reevaluated
periodically and revised in light of changed circumstances. There is no single, permanently valid answer.

PROBABLE CHARACTERISTICS OF FUTURE ARMY ENLISTEES

Until better analyses of population characteristics are made, the following summary of the characteristics of participants in the Army Sample Survey of
Enlistees (April, 1969) may serve as a description of
future Army enlistees:

Racial distribution (percent)

Caucasians	83.3
Negroes	15.3
Others	1.4
	100.0

Geographic origin, all races (percent)

Northeast	15.6
Middle Atlantic	16.4
South	25.2
Midwest	23.9
Far West	19.0
	100.0

Average AFQT scores

All races	54.62
Caucasians	56.77
Negroes	26.11
Others	11.70

Average educational attainment (years in school)

All races	11.70
Caucasians	11.76
Negroes	11.57
Others	10.00

Average age (years)

All races	19.34
Caucasians	19.32
Negroes	19.56
Others	18.44

Marital status (percent unmarried)

All races	83.9
Caucasians	83.3
Negroes	86.9
Others	88.9

Race by geographic distribution (percent)

	Total	N.E.	M.A.	South	M.W.	F.W.
All races	100	15.6	16.4	25.2	23.9	19.0
Caucasians	100	11.7	16.5	24.4	26.1	21.3
Negroes	100	38.4	16.2	25.3	14.1	6.1
Other	100	----	11.1	66.7	----	22.2

This "projection" of population characteristics
of future Army enlistees is very preliminary in nature and statistically unreliable. The survey con-
sisted of approximately 650 enlistees interviewed at
Armed Forces Entrance and Examining Stations. The
sample is not only small but also reflects one particular generation in the waves of generations of
Army enlistees. The characteristics of Army enlistees change over time and under different national
conditions.

CONCLUSIONS

The results of this study indicate that an increase of approximately 38 percent above current pay
will be sufficient to attract enough volunteers to
support a volunteer Army of 858,000 enlisted men. By
comparison with estimates made by earlier studies,
this is a moderate increase. Since in the long run
the overall retention rate in an all-volunteer Army
will be higher than the rate used in this study in
projecting the number of accessions necessary to maintain a force of this size, it is possible that a
force larger than this can be maintained at the pay
level estimated by this study.

The retention rate will be the key factor in
the cost of sustaining a volunteer force. It is
likely that higher pay will more effectively maintain a high retention rate than will some of the incentives which have been suggested to date.

The wage bill of a force of the size required
for limited or all-out war will be very high (even
at the moderate pay rate suggested for a "peacekeeping" force) if every enlisted man receives the same
pay regardless of whether he is an element of the
original force or a newcomer as a result of war.
Since pay differentials among men performing the
same job would create a major morale problem, it may
be necessary to offer variable service contract periods and variable pay geared to the contract period
during time of war. Furthermore, it is believed that
the cost of maintaining a force above a certain size

with an all-volunteer system will be prohibitively
high. Indeed, it may not be possible to meet accession requirements for a very large force with an all-
volunteer system simply by offering higher pay.
Therefore, combinations of incentives and pay should
be devised.

    Civilian wage differentials for different skill
categories will almost certainly persist. This implies that the Army will continue to lose men in certain MOSs to civilian industries unless pay differentials among MOSs are explicitly established. The
most sensible suggestion is that pay be increased on
the basis of MOS rather than increased by the same
amount for all enlisted men.

    The elasticities of enlistment response to
changes in relative military pay calculated in this
study indicate that the Army's elasticity is lower
than that of DOD as a whole. This means that if all
the services pay the same amount under an all-
volunteer system (and other things being equal), the
average enlistment rate for the Army will be lower
than the rate for the other services combined. Therefore, unless the Army wants to be at the short end
of the stick in recruitment, it must either pay more
than the other services or drastically improve its
public image.

    Although the unemployment of civilian males
aged 18-19 may have been an important factor in the
enlistment decision in the past, relying on high unemployment as an acceptable source of volunteers is
not advisable. The long-run future unemployment rate
of this age group will not be significantly different
from what it has been in the recent past. In any
case, most young men who are mentally and physically
qualified will be either in school or fully employed.
Therefore, unless the Army offers pay substantially
higher than the civilian economy does, the quality of
potential enlistees in a time of high unemployment
can be expected to be lower.

    A final word: extreme caution is necessary in
interpreting and implementing the results of a study

such as this. The concept of an all-volunteer military system at a force level of 2.65 million men is new. Estimates and conclusions based on the past are, at best, educated guesswork. The actual cost and sociopolitical impact of an all-volunteer military service cannot be known with accuracy until the country has lived with such a system for some time.

NOTES

1. Science, CLVIII (December 1, 1967), 1139.

2. The Image of the Army: Army Veterans, General Public, High School Educators, and Vietnam Army Veterans in College Appraise the U.S. Army, prepared for N. W. Ayer and Sons, Inc., and the U.S. Army (Princeton, N.J.: Opinion Research Corporation, August, 1969).

3. Anthony C. Fisher, "The Cost of the Draft and the Cost of Ending the Draft," American Economic Review, Vol. LIX, No. 3, June, 1969.

4. Stuart H. Altman, "Earnings, Unemployment, and the Supply of Enlisted Volunteers," The Journal of Human Resources, Vol. 4, No. 1, pp. 38-59, 1969.

5. Fisher, op. cit.

6. Altman, op. cit.

7. See Walter Y. Oi, "The Economic Cost of the Draft--Discussion," American Economic Review, LVII, No. 2 (May, 1967), 39-70; Stuart H. Altman and Alan E. Fechter, "The Supply of Military Personnel in the Absence of a Draft," ibid., 19-31.

8. See Reference Materials from the Department of Defense Study of the Draft, OASD (Manpower) (July, 1966), p. 18.6.

9. Ibid.

10. Ewan Clague, Unemployment--Past, Present, and Future, American Enterprise Institute for Public Policy Research, Analysis No. 12 (June 27, 1969), pp. 44-45.

11. Oi, op. cit.

CHAPTER **5** THE COST AND RELATIVE
EFFECTIVENESS MODEL
FOR ENLISTED PERSONNEL

The quality of an enlisted man depends upon his
contribution to the Army's effectiveness. This
raises the following questions:

1. What is meant by effectiveness?

2. How is it measured?

3. What are the implications for enlisted
   personnel policies?

These questions are considered in the following sections.

EFFECTIVENESS FUNCTION

The effectiveness of enlisted manpower is defined as the utilized potential of a combination of
first-termers and careerists. It is also recognized
that the effectiveness of both first-termers and
careerists depends upon their age, physical and mental condition, educational background, their weapons
and equipment, and other factors. However, it is
reasonable to make the following statements:

1. Better equipment increases the effectiveness of both first-termers and careerists,
   in large part equally; therefore their
   relative effectivenesses are not greatly
   affected by omitting equipment in the effectiveness function. Similarly, many other
   things affect the relative effectiveness

of first-termers and careerists very
little, and thus leave the following analysis largely untouched.

2. There is no conclusive evidence that a
    certain age-and-education mix will im-
    prove overall effectiveness in a syste-
    matic way; soldiership is acquired largely
    by discipline and training while serving.
    On-the-job training is one of the impor-
    tant elements of mastery of soldiership.

3. The physical and mental condition of an
    individual enlisted man is the most ob-
    vious requirement for being an effective
    soldier. Because of this requirement,
    every enlisted man in service is carefully
    screened before being inducted.

It is plausible to assume that the level of experience of enlisted men, as expressed by their years
of service, reflects their training, both formal and
on-the-job, and is therefore the decisive determinant
of their relative effectiveness. This assumption is
more appreciated when one considers the difficulty
of gathering data on the age, education, and equipment of enlisted men. (In later sections, the im-
pacts of technological change are introduced into the
effectiveness function in order to incorporate those
effects of changing equipment type which do not affect
the relative effectiveness of first-termers and careerists.)

Therefore, the effectiveness of enlisted manpower is assumed to be determined by the mix of first-
termers and careerists in a given force. This mix,
in turn, is assumed to depend upon the relative marginal productivities (or marginal rates of effectiveness) of first-termers and careerists. These assumptions are also made for each MOS. Since effectiveness
is never an input, it need not be measurable. However,
it is a calculated output of the models. In this
context, it must be understood to be an index which
differs from true effectiveness by a constant multi-
plier. Such an index is useful for solving many
problems.

In the following text, the use of some calculus is unavoidable in order to preserve the sequence of the model formulations. A reader who wants to accept the results in the sections below without necessarily following the equations can simply overlook them. Verbal explanations precede or follow an equation whenever it is necessary to preserve continuity of the analysis. Proofs and certain details are given elsewhere.[1]

Basic Model

Suppose that effectiveness is a function of the number of first-termers and the number of careerists in the trained base (those who have completed basic training). Assume, also, that adding either a first-termer or a careerist to this trained base increases effectiveness at a decreasing rate. That is, assume that the marginal productivities of both first-termers and careerists are always positive and decreasing as either of them is added to the trained base. The wage of a first-termer is defined as the sum of his basic pay and allowances, other benefits, and costs that might be different from those of a careerist. The wage of a careerist is similarly defined. Details on the wage data used are given in Chapter 2. The following notation is used:

E is effectiveness of the Army

F is number of first-termers in trained base

C is number of careerists in trained base

p is a shadow price per unit of the Army's effectiveness if it were to maximize the level of effectiveness by varying the number of first-termers and careerists, given the total wage cost of all enlisted men

r_F is wage of a first-termer: basic pay and allowances, benefits in kind,

annuities, veterans' benefits (dis-
counted), and other costs

r_C is wage of a careerist: basic pay
and allowances, benefits in kind, annuities, veterans' benefits (discount-
ed), and other costs

ω r_C/r_F, wage of a careerist divided by
wage of a first-termer

$G(.)$ is an effectiveness function which is
homogeneous of degree one and which has
positive first derivatives and negative
second derivatives--i.e., if increases
in both first-termers and careerists
are in the same proportion, effectiveness is also increased by the same
proportion

e is E/C

f is F/C

$g(f)$ is $G(f,1)$

$g'(f)$ is first derivative of g (a small change
in g resulting from a small change in f)

The effectiveness function described above can be
written as

(1) $E = G(F, C)$

The assumptions can be written in the following forms:

(2) $\partial G/\partial F$ and $\partial G/\partial C > 0$; $\partial^2 G/\partial F^2$ and $\partial^2 G/\partial C^2 < 0$

(3) $E = G(F,C) = CG(F/C,1)$

(4) $e = g(f)$

The statements made in (2) assume that the marginal productivity of either first-termers or careerists is increasing at a decreasing rate. Equations

(3) and (4) show the assumption that the function G is homogeneous of degree one--i.e., if the number of both first-termers and careerists changes proportionately, the level of effectiveness changes in the same proportion. Equation (4) is the more convenient normalization (each side divided by C) of Equation (1) because of the assumption of homogeneity.

If the Army minimizes total wage cost given a certain level of effectiveness, or maximizes effectiveness given a certain level of wage cost, it can be shown that the wage ratio   is equal to the ratio of the careerists' marginal productivity to the first-termers' marginal productivity:

(5)
$$\omega = \frac{\partial G/\partial C}{\partial G/\partial F}$$

It can also be shown that the shadow price p can be calculated by dividing either wage by its corresponding marginal productivity:

(6)
$$p = \frac{r_F}{\partial G/\partial F} = \frac{r_C}{\partial G/\partial C}$$

Assumption (3) and Equation (5) imply that

(7)
$$\omega = \frac{g(f)}{g'(f)} - f$$

Equation (7) states that, given the effectiveness function and the wage ratio, the optimal ratio of first-termers to careerists (i.e., optimal in the sense that the ratio is compatible with the existing wage structure) is uniquely determined. This relationship is also presented in Figure 5. The wage-optimal f is denoted by f*. A practical application of Equation (7) is that, given the wage ratio, it is best for the Army to adjust the ratio of first-termers and careerists in the inventory along the wage-optimal ratio f*.

FIGURE 5

The Relationship Between the Wage-Optimal f
Ratio and the Wage Ratio

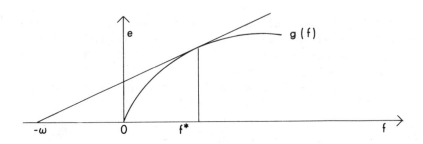

The first derivative of g(f), evaluated at the point
where the ratio f equals the wage-optimal ratio f*,
is apparent from Equation (7):

(8) $g'(f*) = \dfrac{g(f*)}{\omega + f*}$

An explicit solution for f* is obtained from Equation
(8).

It can also be shown that the change in the
wage-optimal f ratio induced by a change in the wage
ratio is always in the same direction because of assumption (2). This means that a relative increase
in the wage ratio in favor of careerists will increase the optimal ratio of first-termers to careerists.

As an immediate application of what has been developed so far, the growth path generated by the effectiveness function is shown below. When the net
rate of change in careerists is constant at θ and the
instantaneous loss rate of first-termers is μ, then
the growth process, under the assumptions described
below, can be formulated in the following differential equations:

(9)
$$\frac{\dot{F}}{F} = \psi g'(f) - \mu$$

(10)
$$\frac{\dot{C}}{C} = \theta$$

A dot above a variable denotes a time derivative, e.g., $\dot{F} = \frac{dF(t)}{dt}$.

A number of assumptions are implicit in these equations. Suppose that an annual increment of first-termers is a fraction of total effectiveness. More specifically, the current increment is some factor, ψ (which is a policy variable), times the total contribution made by the first-termers in the previous year to that year's total effectiveness. Since the effectiveness function is homogeneous of degree one (constant returns to scale), the total effectiveness is exhausted by the sum of the first-termers' marginal effectiveness multiplied by their number and the careerists' marginal effectiveness multiplied by their number.

In mathematical form,

(11)
$$E = \frac{\partial G}{\partial F} F + \frac{\partial G}{\partial C} C$$

Therefore, if the proportion of the first-termers' share in total effectiveness is stated as

(12)
$$s = \frac{E - \frac{\partial G}{\partial C} C}{E}$$

then an annual increment to first-termers is expressed as ψ times their share of total effectiveness:

(13)
$$\dot{F} = \Psi s E = \Psi \frac{\partial G}{\partial F} F$$

Now the rate of change of first-termers, $\dot{F}/F$, is expressed as

(14)
$$\frac{\dot{F}}{F} = \Psi \frac{\partial G}{\partial F} = \Psi g'(f)$$

If the instantaneous loss rate of first-termers is
subtracted from both sides of (14), Equation (9) is
obtained. The factor Ψ is a procurement policy variable for a given level of effectiveness. Equation
(9) now reads as follows: Given the ratio of first-
termers to careerists, the rate of change in first-
termers equals a constant Ψ times the marginal effectiveness of first-termers less the instantaneous loss
rate of first-termers.

Since the rate of change in the ratio of first-
termers to careerists is the rate of change in first-
termers minus the rate of change in careerists, e.g.,

$$(15) \qquad \frac{\dot{f}}{f} = \frac{\dot{F}}{F} - \frac{\dot{C}}{C}$$

Equations (9) and (10) imply that the rate of change
in the ratio of first-termers to careerists equals
a constant Ψ times the marginal effectiveness less
the sum of the rate of careerists' change and first-
termers' loss rate:

$$(16) \qquad \frac{\dot{f}}{f} = \Psi\, g'(f) - \theta - \mu$$

In Equation (8) it was shown that the wage-optimal
ratio of first-termers to careerists is a function
of the wage ratio ω . Therefore, given the wage
ratio and the policy variable Ψ , the rate of change
in the ratio f is uniquely determined in Equation
(16) when the first-termers' loss rate and the rate
of change of careerists are known. This means that
there exists a rational policy for the Army in determining the ratio of first-termers to careerists whenever the wage ratio is specified. Such a ratio f
was previously denoted by f*, the wage-optimal ratio.
A ratio f will be called a balanced career ratio if
$\dot{f}/f = 0$ (i.e., if there is no change in the career
ratio) and will be denoted by $\hat{f}$. Then, Equation (16)
becomes

$$(17) \qquad g'(\hat{f}) = \frac{\theta + \mu}{\Psi}$$

If $\hat{f}$ is the same as f*, then the wage ratio ω for
such f implies a dynamic equilibrium and can be written $\hat{\omega}$.

In order to demonstrate the use of the growth path generated by the effectiveness function and its implications for practical applications, a sample problem is discussed below. Suppose that the effectiveness function is one specified in Equation (23), i.e.,

$$E = K F^{1-\beta} C^{\beta}$$

Then Equation (11) becomes

(11a) $E = F[(1-\beta)KF^{-\beta}C^{\beta}] + C\left(\beta KF^{1-\beta}C^{\beta-1}\right)$

$$= (1-\beta) E + \beta E$$

Now, s (the share of first-termers in total effectiveness) equals $1-\beta$.

The rate of change in first-termers, as defined in the differential equation of (9) is now expressed by

(9a) $\dfrac{\dot{F}}{F} = \Psi K (1-\beta)\ f^{-\beta} - \mu$

From Equations (10) and (15), the rate of change in the ratio of first-termers to careerists expressed by Equation (16) becomes

(16a) $\dfrac{\dot{f}}{f} = \Psi K\ (1-\beta)\ f^{-\beta} - \mu - \theta$

In order to derive the value of Ψ which is compatible with f* (the wage-optimal f ratio) and with $\hat{f}$ (a balanced f ratio), the following two assumptions are made:

1. No change in the ratio f (i.e., $\dot{f}/f = 0$)

2. The ratio f is maintained at the wage-optimal ratio f* (i.e., f = f*).

Now we have the desired value of Ψ under the above two assumptions:

$$\Psi = \frac{\theta + \mu}{K(1-\beta)}\ f*^{\beta}$$

Substitution of Ψ into (9a) gives

(9b) $$\frac{\dot{F}}{F} = (\theta + \mu) \left(\frac{f*}{f}\right)^{\beta} - \mu$$

Equation (9b) states that in order to maintain the
ratio of first-termers to careerists at the wage-
optimal ratio, the net rate of change in first-
termers must equal the sum of the rate of careerists'
change and first-termers' loss rate times an adjustment factor (which is the ratio of the wage-optimal
career ratio to the actual career ratio) less the
first-termers' loss rate. It is easily seen that if
the ratios f* and f are the same, the rate of increment of first-termers must be the rate of net change
in careerists.

In summary, given a wage ratio of first-termers
to careerists, the Army's policy of maintaining the
ratio of first-termers to careerists at the wage-
optimal ratio must be adjusted by the relative gap
between the wage-optimal ratio f* and the actual
ratio f. It will be shown in the section on determination of the effectiveness function that the effectiveness function (i.e., the Cobb-Douglas function)
used in this study uniquely determines the wage-
optimal ratio of first-termers to careerists, given
their wage ratio.

Assuming that the reader thus far accepts the
development of the model presented in this section
without having seen the necessary details which follow in later sections, an illustration using a numerical example is given below.

The following example uses the actual fiscal
1967 data for career field 23 (Missile Fire Control
Electronic Maintenance). We have, for that career
field, the following information:

1.   The calculated wage-optimal ratio of
     first-termers to careerists is f* = .3951

2.   The actual ratio of first-termers to
     careerists in fiscal 1967 is f = .8850

3.   The desired career content ratio (the
     share of careerists in total effectiveness)
     is $\beta = .8184$.

Assume the annual values for θ (the net rate of
change in careerists) and μ (the loss rate of first-
termers) to be 5 percent and 17 percent, respectively.
Then, from Equation (9b) we obtain

$$\frac{\dot{F}}{F} = (.05 + .17) \left(\frac{.3951}{.8850} \right)^{.8184} - .17$$

$$= .1137 - .17$$

$$= - .0563$$

This result means that in order to maintain the
tio of first-termers to careerists at the rate at
which it is wage-optimal when the wage ratio and the
values of θ and μ are given, the Army must decrease
the size of first-termers by 5.6 percent.

Maximum Career Premium

Suppose that the marginal effectiveness of a
careerist is greater than that of a first-termer:

$$\partial G/\partial C > \partial G/\partial F$$

Then, in order to maintain a given level of effectiveness when a careerist leaves, the Army must replace the careerist with a number of first-termers
equal to the ratio of the marginal effectiveness of
a careerist to that of a first-termer. The marginal
wage cost to the Army is the wage cost of a first-
termer times the ratio of the rates of marginal effectiveness, less the wage cost of a careerist. The
same effectiveness can be obtained by paying additional money to a reenlistee, up to an amount, called
the maximum career premium (MCP), which is above the
marginal wage cost when the careerist is replaced by
first-termers:

(18) $MCP = \dfrac{\partial G/\partial C}{\partial G/\partial F} r_F - r_C = r_C \left(\dfrac{\partial G/\partial C}{\partial G/\partial F} \dfrac{1}{\omega} - 1 \right)$

Paying a careerist the premium is equivalent to in-
curring a higher cost for careerists, which is

(19) $r_C + MCP = \dfrac{\partial G/\partial C}{\partial G/\partial F} \; r_F$

The ratio of the new careerists' wage to the old is

(20) $\dfrac{r_C + MCP}{r_C} = \dfrac{\partial G/\partial C}{\partial G/\partial F} \; \dfrac{1}{\omega}$

If the Army's compensation policy has already mini-
mized wage cost, the maximum career premium is zero.
It is clear from Equation (20) that this is true if
and only if the wage ratio equals the ratio of the
two rates of marginal effectiveness, i.e., the ratio
f is wage-optimal.

Determination of the Effectiveness Function

So far the marginal effectiveness of both first-
termers and careerists has been discussed without
specifying the nature of the effectiveness function.
The major difficulty in constructing such a function
is that no data meaningful to the function can be
found on the index of utilized potential. This means
that the parameters of the function cannot be estimated by using conventional statistical methods, because there are no data for the variable in the left-
hand side of the effectiveness function.

Suppose it is known that for a given MOS, some
constant times the difference between the marginal
effectiveness of a careerist and that of a first-
termer depends linearly upon the career content ratio
as stated in the following equation:

(21) $K \left(\dfrac{\partial G}{\partial C} - \dfrac{\partial G}{\partial F} \right) = \dfrac{\beta}{\beta - \alpha} - \dfrac{1}{\beta - \alpha} \, \gamma$

where γ = the career content ratio $\dfrac{C}{C+F}$
           α = the lower limit of γ
           β = the upper limit of γ
           K = some positive constant.

Then, K times the difference between the two rates of
marginal effectiveness is 1 at $\gamma = \alpha$, and 0 at $\gamma = \beta$.

Figure 6 illustrates this relationship.

FIGURE 6

A Linear Relationship Between the Career
Content Ratio and Productivity

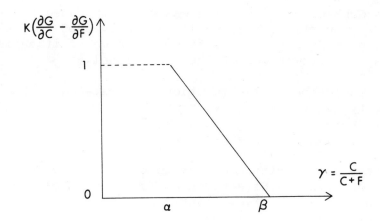

It is clear from the figure that the Army can always
increase total effectiveness by increasing the career
content ratio until it becomes β, at which point the
difference between the two rates of marginal effectiveness is zero. Therefore, any effectiveness function, if it is to be the best in the sense that it
presupposes technical efficiency and states the maximum effectiveness obtainable from every possible
input combination of first-termers and careerists,
must be evaluated at the career content ratio of β.

Now consider the homogeneous Cobb-Douglas function of degree one. This function has the following
properties:

1. It is single-valued and continuous
    everywhere

2. It has continuous first- and second-order
    partial derivatives

3. It is defined for all finite positive inputs

4.   It has constant returns to scale (i.e.,
     if all inputs change proportionately,
     output changes in the same proportion)

5.   It has an infinite number of possible
     input combinations

6.   It has analytical tractability.

This Cobb-Douglas function was chosen because of the
above properties, because it is widely used for an-
alyzing problems of this type, and because it satis-
fies the assumptions of the basic model.

The Cobb-Douglas function of first-degree homogeneity is written

(22) $E = K \, F^{1-b} \, C^{b}$

where K is a positive number to be specified in the
section "Dynamic Effectiveness Model."   It can be
shown that $b = \beta$, i.e., that

(23) $E = K \, F^{1-\beta} C^{\beta}$

(24) $0 < \alpha \leq \gamma \leq \beta < 1$

and the marginal effectiveness of a careerist minus
that of a first-termer is a function of γ and β:

(25) $\dfrac{\partial G}{\partial C} - \dfrac{\partial G}{\partial F} = K \left(\dfrac{1-\gamma}{\gamma}\right)^{-\beta} \left(\dfrac{\beta}{\gamma} - 1\right)$

A graphical presentation of the relation (25) appears
in Figure 7, which shows that a decrease in the differential marginal productivities is associated with
an increase in the career content ratio at a decreasing rate.   The ratio of the marginal effectiveness
of careerists to that of first-termers equals the
ratio of the careerists' share to the first-termers'
share of total wages times the ratio of first-termers
to careerists:

(26) $\dfrac{\partial G/\partial C}{\partial G/\partial F} = \left(\dfrac{\beta}{1-\beta}\right) \left(\dfrac{1-\gamma}{\gamma}\right)$

FIGURE 7

The Differential Marginal Productivities
and the Career Content Ratio

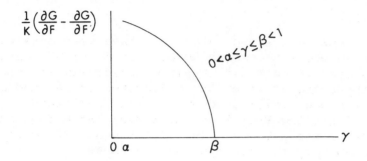

If the career content ratio is actually β, the differential marginal effectiveness in Relation (25)
disappears and the marginal effectiveness ratio in
Relation (26) becomes one. Notice that the phrase
"share of total wages" is used in the description of
the ratio $\beta/(1-\beta)$ in Relation (26). It is always
true that in the Cobb-Douglas function used in this
chapter, β is equal to the careerists' share in the
total wage bill when the f ratio is wage-optimal.
This is because $(1-\beta)+\beta = 1$ (i.e., it has constant
returns to scale).

Before some examples are presented, it should
be mentioned that whenever the actual career content
ratio γ equals the share factor β, we denote such γ
as γ^{**} and call it the technological- or MOS-optimum
career content ratio. Consequently, the actual ratio of first-termers to careerists, f, becomes f^{**} if
$\gamma = \gamma^{**}$, since $f = \frac{1-\gamma}{\gamma}$. In the applications described
in the later sections of this chapter, any variable
which bears the superscript ** is associated with or
optimized with respect to either γ^{**} or f^{**}. As the
reader may recall, the wage-optimal ratio f^*, which
in turn defines γ^*, has been defined. In fact, the
f^* ratio equals the wage ratio of careerists to first-
termers times the inverse of their share ratio:

(27) $$f^* = \omega\left(\frac{1-\beta}{\beta}\right)$$

This means that if their wage ratio is the same as their share ratio, the wage-optimal ratio of first-termers to careerists will be one. As in the case of the variables with two asterisks, any variable which bears the superscript of one asterisk is related to f^* or γ^*.

Data on desired career mix have been obtained from an ODCSPER memorandum of July 12, 1967, entitled "Enlisted Force Mix." Desired career mix is interpreas the ratio at which the difference of the two marginal productivities becomes zero. For example, MOS 68E (Rotor and Propeller Repairman) has a desired career ratio β of .8. The effectiveness function for this MOS may therefore be expressed as

$$E_{MOS68E} = K \, F^{.2} \, C^{.8}$$

Using Relations (25) and (26), the differential marginal productivity is

$$K \left(\frac{1-\gamma}{\gamma}\right)^{-.8} \left(\frac{.8}{\gamma} - 1\right)$$

$$= .723K \qquad\qquad\qquad \gamma = .4$$

$$= .461K \quad\text{when} \qquad\qquad \gamma = .6$$

$$= 0 \qquad\qquad\qquad \gamma = \gamma^{**} = .8$$

and the ratio of the marginal productivities is

$$\left(\frac{.8}{1-.8}\right)\left(\frac{1-\gamma}{\gamma}\right) = 4 \, \frac{1-\gamma}{\gamma}$$

$$= 6 \qquad\qquad\qquad \gamma = .4$$

$$= 2.7 \quad\text{when} \qquad\qquad \gamma = .6$$

$$= 1 \qquad\qquad\qquad \gamma = \gamma^{**} = .8$$

It is desired that these differential productivities and productivity ratios be zero and one, respectively, in order to attain maximum effectiveness. For

practical purposes, either of these two maximum effectiveness criteria can be used. For the reader who
feels that the ratio of the marginal productivities
overstates the phenomenon, the ratio of the MOS-
optimum effectiveness E** (effectiveness function
whose career content ratio is evaluated at the MOS-
optimum career content ratio γ**) to the actual effectiveness E is given below.

$$\frac{E^{**}}{E} = \left(\frac{1-\beta}{1-\gamma}\right)^{1-\beta}\left(\frac{\beta}{\gamma}\right)^{\beta}$$

$$= 1.4 \qquad\qquad \gamma = .4$$

$$= 1.1 \quad\text{when}\quad \gamma = .6 \text{ and } \beta = .8$$

$$= 1 \qquad\qquad \gamma^{**} = \gamma = .8$$

To summarize: this section completes the specifica-
tions of the basic model of the effectiveness function. The data on desired career mix will be used as
the value of β in the actual application of the effectiveness model.

Dynamic Effectiveness Model

The purpose of the dynamic effectiveness model
described in this section is to show changes in effectiveness over a time period. It uses the same
basic effectiveness function that has already been
developed, but all the variables are now time-
dependent. Also considered in this model are technological change, $A(t)$, and variations in quality ($Q[\rho]$)
due to different rates of change (ρ) of the trained
base. The major assumptions are the following:

1.   Technology and quality are neutral in the
     sense that the ratio of the marginal ef-
     fectiveness of first-termers to that of
     careerists remains constant regardless of
     changes in technology and quality if the
     career content ratio remains constant

2.   Effectiveness decreases as the rate of
     change ρ increases

3.   The quality index approaches zero as the
     rate of change ρ approaches infinity, and
     unity as the rate approaches zero.

The second assumption needs an explanation. Effectiveness is always increasing when either a first-
termer or a careerist (or both) is (are) added to the
trained base. This is due to the assumption made in
(2). However, changes in the size of the trained
base always cause disruptions and some adjustment
problems within the Army which tend to lower quality
$Q(\rho)$ and, therefore, to lower an otherwise obtainable level of effectiveness.

When E (effectiveness), F (number of first-
termers), C (number of careerists), and other variables defined in previous sections are replaced by
E(t), F(t), C(t), etc., the basic Equation (1), now
using the first assumption above, can be written as

(28) $E(t) = H(F(t), C(t); \rho, t)$

                         $= A(t) \, Q(\rho) G(F(t), C(t))$

It is assumed that

(29) $\dfrac{dQ(\rho)}{d\rho} < 0$

(30) $\lim_{\rho \to \pm\infty} Q(\rho) = 0$ and $\lim_{\rho \to 0} Q(\rho) = 1$

where

(31) $\rho = \dfrac{\dfrac{d(F(t) + C(t))}{dt}}{F(t) + C(t)}$

Equation (28) states that effectiveness at time t is
a function of technological change, the quality factor $Q(\rho)$, and input combinations of first-termers and
careerists at time t. The factor K in Equation (23)
is now replaced by the product of A(t) and $Q(\rho)$.
Condition (29) states that the change in quality due
to an increase in the rate of change ρ must be negative. Condition (30) restates the third major

assumption above. The rate of change of the trained
base is defined in (31). This rate is calculated
from the output of the inventory model. It is now
assumed that

$$(32) \qquad Q(\rho) = \frac{1}{e^{|\rho|j}} \qquad (j > 0)$$

This is positive and meets conditions (29) and (30).
It is also assumed that

$$(33) \qquad A(t) = e^{\lambda t}$$

where λ is the rate of technological change. Equation (28) now becomes

$$(34) \qquad E(t) = e^{\lambda t - |\rho(t)| j} \, G(F(t), C(t))$$

If the rate of change ρ is constant over a period,
the current size of the trained base can be determined by the size of the trained base at the beginning of the period (t=0) and by the rate of change:

$$(35) \qquad F(t) = (F(0) + C(0)) \, e^{\rho t} - C(t)$$

Using the above relation, the effectiveness function
(34) is written as

$$(36) \qquad E(t) = e^{\lambda t - |\rho(t)| j} \, G \, [(F(0)$$

$$+ C(0)) \, e^{\rho t} - C(t), \, C(t)]$$

Rewriting Equation (34) in a form comparable
with Equation (4),

$$(34a) \qquad e(t) = e^{\lambda t \, |\rho(t)| j} g(f(t))$$

where $\qquad e(t) = \dfrac{E(t)}{C(t)}$

$$f(t) = \frac{F(t)}{C(t)}$$

$$g(f(t)) = G(f(t), 1)$$

Using the Cobb-Douglas function, Equation (34) becomes

(37) $E(t) = e^{\lambda t- |\rho(t)| j} (F(t))^{1-\beta} (C(t))^{\beta}$

Equation (34a) in the Cobb-Douglas form is

(38) $e(t) = e^{\lambda t- |\rho(t)| j} [f(t)]^{1-\beta}$

The wage ratio now has a more general expression when the f ratio is wage-optimal:

(39) $\omega(t) = \dfrac{g(f^*(t))}{g'(f^*(t))} - f^*(t)$

In terms of the Cobb-Douglas effectiveness function,

(40) $\omega(t) = \dfrac{\beta}{1-\beta} f^*(t)$

The expression for the maximum career premium (MCP) is now

(41) $MCP(t) = \left(\dfrac{f(t)\beta}{1-\beta} - \omega(t) \right) r_F(t)$

The wage ratio ω in Equations (39) through (41) is a given ratio. Therefore, the MCP will be zero if f(t) is wage-optimal. The applications of the model developed in this section are described in later sections of this chapter.

First-Termer Aggregation Model

The purpose of the model described in this section is to show the effect of differences in proficiency among first-termers. It is nearly identical with the model presented in the previous section. The difference is that first-termers are classified by year of service. The first group of first-termers is the first-year first-termers, the second group is the second-year first-termers, and the third group is the third-year first-termers. All others are considered to be careerists. Both first-termers and careerists are identified by MOS or MOS-equivalent occupational areas. (See Tables 12 and 14.) Assuming

that the proficiency (determined by the learning process) of careerists is 100 percent in each MOS, the
number of first-termers in each year of service in
each MOS (area) will be weighted by the relative proficiency rating and then summed over the first three
years of service. This assumption could be modified
by extending the period of the learning process into
the fourth year and beyond. To put it graphically,
the proficiency curve in Figure 8 could go either up
or down after the three-year point. This means that
the proficiency rating of careerists in each MOS
(area) could be other than 100 percent at any point
after the three-year service period.

FIGURE 8

The Proficiency Curve of Each MOS

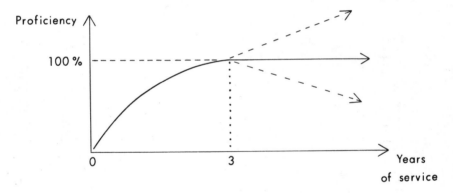

Table 12 is based on the original assumption
(i.e., the solid line in Figure 8). In this table,
F denotes the number of first-termers. The first
subscript indicates an MOS; the second, the year of
service. The quantities a, b, and c are proficiency
ratings relative to those of careerists, which are
always 100 percent.

We define

(42) $$\overline{F}_k(t) = \frac{a_k \ F_{k,1}(t) + b_k \ F_{k,2}(t) + c_k \ F_{k,3}(t)}{b_k}$$

TABLE 15

Proficiency of First-Termers Relative to
Careerists, by MOS

MOS	First-Termers						Careerists 4th Year and Up	
	1st Year		2nd Year		3rd Year			
	Proficiency	Number	Proficiency	Number	Proficiency	Number	Proficiency	Number
1	a_1	F_{11}	b_1	F_{12}	c_1	F_{13}	100%	c_1
2	a_2	F_{21}	b_2	F_{22}	c_2	F_{23}	100%	c_2
· · · · ·	·	·	·	·	·	·	·	·
k	a_k	F_{k1}	b_k	F_{k2}	c_k	F_{k3}	100%	c_k
· · · · ·	·	·	·	·	·	·	·	·
K	a_K	F_{K1}	b_K	F_{K2}	c_K	F_{K3}	100%	c_K

Source: Table is based on Figure 8.

where $F_{k,1}^{(t)}$ is the number of first-year first-termers in the kth MOS

$F_{k,2}^{(t)}$ is the number of second-year first-termers in the kth MOS

$F_{k,3}^{(t)}$ is the number of third-year first-termers in the kth MOS

a_k is the proficiency rating of a first-year first-termer in the kth MOS

b_k is the proficiency rating of a second-year first-termer in the kth MOS

c_k is the proficiency rating of a third-year first-termer in the kth MOS.

$\overline{F}_k^{(t)}$ in Equation (42) is the second-year equivalent of all first-termers, i.e., that number of second-year first-termers whose total proficiency is the same as the proficiency of all first-termers in the kth MOS. The variable $\overline{F}_k^{(t)}$ will be called the "first-termers aggregation." It is a weighted average of all first-termers, the weights being the relative proficiency.

The sum of the first-termers aggregation over all MOSs is

(43) $\quad \overline{F}(t) = \sum_k \overline{F}_k(t)$

The analogue of Equation (28), by substitution of $\overline{F}(t)$ into $F(t)$, is

(44) $\quad \overline{E}(t) = A(t)\, Q(\rho)\, G(\overline{F}(t), C(t))$

For the kth MOS, this effectiveness function would be

(45) $\quad \overline{E}_k^{(t)} = A_k(t)\quad Q(\rho)\, G(\overline{F}_k(t), C_k(t))$

If the function G is the Cobb-Douglas function, Equations (45) and (44) become

(46) $\quad \overline{E}_k^{(t)} = e^{\lambda_k t - |\rho| j} \left(\overline{F}_k^{(t)} \right)^{1-\beta_k} \left(C_k^{(t)} \right)^{\beta_k}$

$$(47) \qquad \overline{E}(t) = e^{\lambda t - |\rho| \, j} \, (\overline{F}(t))^{1-\beta} (C(t))^{\beta}$$

The normalized versions of these two equations are the following:

$$(48) \qquad e_k^{(t)} = e^{\lambda_k t - |\rho| \, j} \left(\overline{f}_{k\,(t)}\right)^{1-\beta_k}$$

$$(49) \qquad e(t) = e^{\lambda t - |\rho| \, j} \, (\overline{f}(t))^{1-\beta}$$

where $\quad \overline{f}_{k\,(t)} = \dfrac{\overline{F}_k^{(t)}}{C_{k\,(t)}}$

and $\qquad \overline{f}(t) = \dfrac{\overline{F}(t)}{C(t)}$

The wage ratio $\omega(t)$ and the maximum career premium (MCP) are now expressed as follows:

$$(50) \qquad \omega(t) = \frac{g(\overline{f}*(t))}{g'(\overline{f}*(t))} - \overline{f}*(t)$$

$$= \frac{\beta}{1-\beta} \, \overline{f}*(t)$$

$$(51) \quad \overline{MCP}(t) = \left(\frac{\beta}{1-\beta} \, \overline{f}(t) - \omega(t)\right) r_F^{(t)}$$

Similar expressions for each MOS are obtained by adding the subscript k to the variables in these two relations.

In later sections, any variable with a superscript bar over the variable is related to "first-termers aggregation."

Aggregation of the Effectiveness Functions

There are 62 two-digit MOS categories and therefore that many effectiveness functions. It is desirable that the effectiveness function for all enlisted men be obtained by aggregating or averaging

the effectiveness functions of the individual MOSs.
There are generally three ways of performing such an
aggregation. The first is to sum the individual effectiveness functions (one for each MOS). The second
is to estimate the overall effectiveness function
without regard to the individual effectiveness function of each MOS. The third is to estimate the overall function by relating each individual MOS effectiveness function to it.

The first method presents no problem. All the
quantities E_1 through E_k (k = number of MOSs) are
added together. The second method presents a problem because neither the data to estimate the parameters nor the knowledge of the relationship between
the overall career content ratio and overall productivity is available. Therefore, the third method is
discussed below.

Consider a microrelation within a given MOS:

$$(52) \qquad y_k = f_k \ (x_{1_K}, \ldots, x_{v_k}, \ldots, x_{v_K}) \qquad \begin{matrix} k = 1, \ldots, K \\ v = 1, \ldots, V \end{matrix}$$

The problem is to find a function F such that

$$(53) \qquad y = F \ (x_1, \ldots, x_V)$$

where Y and the X_V are defined by the aggregating
functions of

$$(54) \qquad y = y \ (y_1, \ldots, y_k, \ldots, y_K)$$

$$(55) \qquad X_v = X_v \ (X_{v_1}, \ldots, X_{v_k}, \ldots, X_{v_K}) \qquad v = 1, \ldots, V$$

A set of K equations in (52) can be considered
as individual MOS effectiveness functions. These
functions are a set of microrelations. The macro-
relation (53) is what is sought. The basic difficulty is consistency among the three elements of the
problem: microrelation, aggregation of variables--
i.e., the aggregation in (54) and (55)--and macro-
relation. The purpose of this section is to develop a
consistent and unbiased method of aggregation despite

some drawbacks of such a method. Other available methods are not considered.

There are two major cases of the aggregation problem:

1. The exponents, the β_k, in the effectiveness functions, are the same in every MOS.

2. There are at least two different exponents.

In Case 1, an aggregate Cobb-Douglas function is justified either as (a) the only aggregate function which is perfect under optimal assignment* and under free transferability from one MOS to another or as (b) the function which gives, on the average, the correct marginal rate of substitution between two aggregates (overall first-termers and overall careerists) under reasonable assignment rules. There is no problem of averaging individual MOS effectiveness functions. In Case 2, perfect aggregation is not possible even under optimal assignment and free transferability without having further information which amounts to the knowledge required in the previously mentioned second method of aggregation. Therefore, an approximation procedure is used. This approximation will be better if the individual exponents, the β_k, are not very different from each other, for the reason stated in Case 1.

For aggregation of effectiveness functions under Case 2, a method developed by Morton and Fisher is used.[2] For the kth MOS, the Cobb-Douglas effectiveness function (23) is

(56) $E_k = K_k \, F_k^{1-\beta_k} C_k^{\beta_k}$ $(k=1,\ldots,K)$

This function implies that, at a given level of effectiveness, the marginal trade-off between

---

*Optimal assignment is assignment such that the marginal product of a first-termer or careerist is the same in every MOS.

first-termers and careerists is

(57) $$\left(\frac{\partial F_k}{\partial C_k}\right)_{E_k} = \text{constant} = -\frac{\beta_k}{1-\beta_k}\frac{F_k}{C_k}$$

The percentage increase in F_k that compensates for a
1 percent decrease in C_k is thus constant at $\beta_k/(1-\beta_k)$.
In terms of absolute numbers of men, the number of
first-termers that must be added to compensate for the
loss of one careerist is proportional to the ratio in
the kth MOS of first-termers to careerists. Let N_k
denote the left-hand side of Equation (57):

(58) $$N_k = -\frac{\beta_k}{1-\beta_k}f_k$$

where $f_k = F_k/C_k$. Consider the quantity N_k^*:

(59) $$N_k^* = -\frac{\beta}{1-\beta}f_k$$

It is assumed that

(60) $$N_k = N_k^* \, e^{\epsilon_k}$$

where ϵ_k is a randomly distributed error with zero
mean and constant variance distributed independently
of MOS and uncorrelated with N_k. Let d_k denote
$\beta_k/(1-\beta_k)$ and let d denote $\beta/(1-\beta)$. Then,

(61) $$d_k = de^{\epsilon_k}$$

Taking logarithms,

(62) $$\ln d = \ln d_k - \epsilon_k \qquad k=1,\ldots,K$$

The $\ln d$ is estimated by taking a weighted average of
the $\ln d_k$, the weights being the number of men in each
MOS. Let $S_k = C_k + F_k$ be the total number of men in
the kth MOS and let $S = \sum_{k=1}^{K} S_k$ be the total number of
men in all MOSs. The estimator of $\ln d$ is then

(63) $$\ln d = \frac{\sum_k S_k \ln d_k}{S}$$

This is a linear estimator of $\ln d$. Since ϵ_k has
zero mean, it is also unbiased. Estimator (63) can

be rewritten

$$\ln \hat{d} = \sum_k \frac{S_k}{S} \left(\ln d_K\right)$$

or

(64) $$\hat{d} = d_1^{(S_1/S)}, \ldots, d_k^{(S_K/S)}$$

Thus $\hat{d}$ is a weighted geometric average of d_k of the
individual MOS effectiveness functions in (56). It
is shown in the paper by Morton and Fisher cited
above that the use of the estimator in (64) can be
justified on considerably more than intuitive grounds.

Now $\hat{\beta}$ is obtained from $\hat{d}$. Then the estimate of
the tradeoff between all first-termers and all careerists in the total number of enlisted men is

(65) $$-\left(\frac{\partial F}{\partial C}\right)_{E \, = \, constant} = \frac{\hat{\beta}}{1-\hat{\beta}} \; \frac{F}{C}$$

Analysis of Cost Effectiveness Ratio

The following analysis can be applied either to
an MOS or to all enlisted men. The ratio of cost to
effectiveness is

(66) $$\frac{\text{Cost}}{\text{Effectiveness}} = \frac{\text{F (unit cost of first-termers)} + \text{C (unit cost of careerists)}}{\text{E (unit price of effectiveness)}}$$

where

cost = all elements of training and
       maintenance

price = a shadow price

The shadow price, a make-believe price rather than
market price, should be a price such that if the Army
were to maximize its effectiveness subject to a budget constraint, it would arrive at the wage optimum

described above. This price (p) was given in Equation (6):

$$p = \frac{r_F}{\partial G/\partial F} = \frac{r_C}{\partial G/\partial C}$$

If the Army is not at the wage optimum, (6) does not hold, and the shadow price generated by first-termers is not equated to the shadow price generated by careerists:

(67)
$$\frac{r_F}{\partial G/\partial F} \neq \frac{r_C}{\partial G/\partial C}$$

In this case, each shadow price and the ratio of the first to the second are calculated. This ratio is the right-hand side of Equation (20):

$$\frac{r_C + MCP}{r_C} = \frac{\partial G/\partial C}{\partial G/\partial F} \quad \frac{1}{\omega}$$

In each case the deviation of the ratio from 1 is a measure of the deviation from the wage optimum. In the calculation of the cost-effectiveness ratios, the shadow price (p) is set equal to one, which merely changes the units of the ratios.

Equations Calculated

It is evident that many calculations can be made on the basis of the models of this chapter. The table below lists the equations used in such calculations, which are performed by a computer program. The range of t is from fiscal 1969 to fiscal 1980. Wherever possible, the notations used below are identical to those used in previous sections. New symbols are explained. For convenience, the time variable t is a subscript instead of being placed in parentheses. The subscript k denotes the kth MOS. A variable without the k subscript refers to all enlisted men. It should also be noted that the subscripts F and C have been replaced by f and c.

TABLE 16

Equations Calculated by Relative Cost and Effectiveness Model

Rate of change in inventory

$$(1)\quad \rho_t = (I_{t+1} - I_t)/I_t^{\,a}$$

Combined changes in technology and quality

$$(2)\quad K_{k,t} = e^{(\lambda_k t - |\rho_t| j)}$$

Career content ratio

$$(3)\quad \gamma_{k,t}$$

Ratio of first-termers to careerists

$$(4)\quad f_{k,t} = (1 - \gamma_{k,t})/\gamma_{k,t}$$

Actual effectiveness

$$(5)\quad E_{k,t} = K_{k,t}\, I_{k,t}\, (1 - \gamma_{k,t})^{(1-\beta_k)}\, \gamma_{k,t}^{\beta_k,t}$$

MOS-optimum effectiveness

$$(6)\quad E^{**}_{k,t} = K_{k,t}\, I_{k,\underline{t}}\, (1-\beta_k)^{(1-\beta_k)}\, \beta_k^{\beta_k}$$

Ratio of wage-optimum to MOS-optimum effectiveness

$$(7)\quad E^{*}_{k,t}/E^{**}_{k,t} = \omega_{k,t}^{(1-\beta_k)}/[\beta_k + \omega_{k,t}^{(1-\beta_k)}]$$

Wage-optimum effectiveness

$$(8)\quad E^{*}_{k,t} = (E^{*}_{k,t}/E^{**}_{k,t})\, E^{**}_{k,t}$$

Ratio of actual to wage-optimum effectiveness

$$(9)\quad E_{k,t}/E^{*}_{k,t}$$

Ratio of actual to MOS-optimum effectiveness

(10) $E_{k,t}/E_{k,t}^{**}$

Aggregate ratio of shares in effectiveness, careerists to first-termers

(11) $d_{f,c,t} = e^{[\sum_k I_{k,t} \log_e (\beta_k/(1-\beta_k))/I_t]}$

Aggregate share in effectiveness for careerists

(12) $\beta_t = d_{f,c,t}/(1+d_{f,c,t})$

Aggregate wage ratio of careerists to first-termers

(13) $\omega_t = \dfrac{(\sum_k r_{c,k,t}\, \gamma_{k,t}I_{k,t})/\gamma_t}{(\sum_k r_{f,k,t}(1-\gamma_{k,t})I_{k,t})/(1-\gamma_t)}$

Relations (2) through (10) replaced by an aggregate

(14) Replace λ_k by λ; $(1-\gamma_{k,t})$ by $(1-\gamma_t)$;

$I_{k,t}$ with I_t; β_k by β_t; and $\omega_{k,t}$ by ω_t

in equations (2) through (10), thus producing

K_t; γ_t; f_t; E_t; E_t^{**}; E_t/E_t^{**}; E_t^*; E_t/E_t^*; E_t/E_t^{**}

Sum of effectiveness over MOSs

(15) $EE_t = \sum_k E_{k,t}$

Sum of wage-optimum effectiveness over MOSs

(16) $EE_t^* = \sum_k E_{k,t}^*$

(cont.)

151

TABLE 16 (cont.)

Equations Calculated by Relative Cost and Effectiveness Model

Sum of MOS-optimum effectiveness over MOSs

(17) $EE_t^{**} = \sum_k E_{k,t}^{**}$

Marginal tradeoff between first-termers and careerists

(18) $N_{k,t} = f_{k,t} \, \beta_k / (1-\beta_k)$

Maximum career premium

(19) $MCP_{k,t} = (N_{k,t} - \omega_{k,t}) \, r_{f,k,t}$

Calculated price per unit of effectiveness from first-termers' wage policy

(20) $P_{f,k,t} = r_{f,k,t} \, f_{k,t}^{\beta_k} \Big/ \left[K_{k,t}^{(1-\beta_k)} \right]$

Calculated price per unit of effectiveness from careerists' wage policy

(21) $P_{c,k,t} = r_{c,k,t} \Big/ \left[\beta_k \, K_{k,t} \, f_{k,t}^{(1-\beta_k)} \right]$

Ratio of calculated prices

(22) $P_{k,t} = P_{f,k,t} \Big/ P_{c,k,t}$ [b]

Shadow price per unit of effectiveness

(23) $P_{c,k,t}^* = P_{f,k,t}^*$

$= r_{f,k,t} \, \omega_{k,t}^{\beta_k} \Big/ \left[K_{k,t} (1-\beta_k)^{(1-\beta_k)} \beta_k^{\beta_k} \right]$

Wage-optimum ratio of first-termers to careerists

(24) $f_{k,t}^* = \omega_{k,t} \left[(1-\beta_k)/\beta_k \right]$

(cont.)

Wage-optimum career content ratio   (25) $\gamma_{k,t}^* = 1/(1+f_{k,t}^*)$

Actual total wage cost   (26) $C_{k,t} = (1-\gamma_{k,t}) I_{k,t} r_{f,k,t} + \gamma_{k,t} I_{k,t} r_{c,k,t}$

Wage-optimum total wage cost   (27) $C_{k,t}^* = (1-\gamma_{k,t}^*) I_{k,t} r_{f,k,t} + \gamma_{k,t}^* I_{k,t} r_{c,k,t}$

MOS-optimum total wage cost   (28) $C_{k,t}^{**} = (1-\beta_k) I_{k,t} r_{f,k,t} + \beta_k I_{k,t} r_{c,k,t}$

Actual cost-effectiveness ratio   (29) $CF_{k,t} = C_{k,t}/E_{k,t}$

Wage-optimum cost-effectiveness ratio   (30) $CF_{k,t}^* = C_{k,t}^*/E_{k,t}^*$

MOS-optimum cost-effectiveness ratio   (31) $CF_{k,t}^{**} = C_{k,t}^{**}/E_{k,t}^{**}$

Enlisted men's total wage cost   (32) $C_t = \sum_k C_{k,t}$

Enlisted men's wage-optimum total wage cost   (33) $C_t^* = \sum_k C_{k,t}^*$

Enlisted men's MOS-optimum total wage cost   (34) $C_t^{**} = \sum_k C_{k,t}^{**}$

153

TABLE 16 (cont.)

Equations Calculated by Relative Cost and Effectiveness Model

Enlisted men's actual total cost-effectiveness	(35)	$CF_t = C_t/EE_t$
Enlisted men's wage-optimum total cost-effectiveness	(36)	$CF_t^* = C_t^*/EE_t^{**}$
Enlisted men's MOS-optimum total cost-effectiveness	(37)	$CF_t^{**} = C_t^{**}/EE_t^{**}$
Total training cost	(38)	$CI_{k,t} = I_{k,t}\,TC_{k,t}^c$
Total actual cost	(39)	$C'_{k,t} = C_{k,t} + CI_{k,t}$
Wage-optimum total cost	(40)	$C'^*_{k,t} = C^*_{k,t} + CI_{k,t}$
MOS-optimum total cost	(41)	$C'^{**}_{k,t} = C^{**}_{k,t} + CI_{k,t}$
Relations (29) through (37) replaced by total cost, thus forming enlisted men's actual total cost, including training cost	(42)	Replace $C_{k,t}$ by $C'_{k,t}$; $C^*_{k,t}$ by $C'^*_{k,t}$; and $C^{**}_{k,t}$ with $C'^{**}_{k,t}$ in Equations (29)-(37), thus forming $CF'_{k,t}$; $CF'^*_{k,t}$; $CF'^{**}_{k,t}$; C'_t; etc.

First-termers aggregation

$$(43)\quad \bar{F}_{k,t} = \frac{a_j(k) A_{k,t} + b_j(k) z_{k,t}(1-\gamma_{k,t}) I_{k,t}}{b_j(k)}$$

$$+ \frac{c_j(k)(1-z_{k,t}-n_{k,t}) f_{k,t} I_{k,t}}{b_j(k)}{}^d$$

Career content ratio adjusted by first-termers aggregation

$$(44)\quad \bar{\gamma}_{k,t} = \gamma_{k,t} I_{k,t} / \left[\bar{F}_{k,t} + (\gamma_{k,t}) I_{k,t}\right]$$

Ratio of first-termers to careerists adjusted by first-termers aggregation

$$(45)\quad \bar{f}_{k,t} = (1-\bar{\gamma}_{k,t}) / \bar{\gamma}_{k,t}$$

Inventory adjusted by first-termers aggregation

$$(46)\quad \bar{I}_{k,t} = \bar{F}_{k,t} + \gamma_{k,t} I_{k,t}$$

Aggregate career content ratio adjusted by first-termers aggregation

$$(47)\quad \bar{\gamma}_t = \sum_k (\gamma_{k,t} I_{k,t} / \sum_k (\gamma_{k,t} I_{k,t} + \bar{F}_{k,t})$$

Relations (5) through (42) adjusted by first-termers aggregation

(48) Replace $I_{k,t}$ by $\bar{I}_{k,t}$; $f_{k,t}$ by $\bar{f}_{k,t}$; and $\gamma_{k,t}$ by $\bar{\gamma}_{k,t}$ and repeat Equations (5) through (42).

(cont.)

155

TABLE 16 (cont.)

$^a I_t$ is total inventory, which equals careerist plus first-termers.

^{b}A comment on Equation (22) is needed. It can easily be shown that in order to make $P_{k,t}$ (the ratio of the price generated by first-termers' wage policy to that generated by careerists' wage policy) equal to one, at which the wage policy for both first-termers and careerists is optimum, either of the following conditions must be met:

1. The actual ratio of first-termers to careerists equals the wage-optimum ratio of the same (e.g., $f_k = f_k^*$)

2. The weighted average of wages for first-termers equals that for careerists (e.g., $r_{f,k} = r_{c,k}$).

The purpose of Equation (22) is to show the evidence of a sub-optimum wage policy.

$^c TC_{k,t}$ is training cost per enlisted man in an MOS

$^d A_{k,t}$ is the number of accessions by MOS = $F_{k,1}^{(t)}$ in "First-Termer Aggregation Model"

$I_{k,t}$ is the inventory by MOS

$z_{k,t}$ is the proportion of first-termers who are in the second year in each MOS

$n_{k,t}$ is the proportion of first-termers who are in the first year in each MOS

156

DATA

Data inputs necessary for calculation of the equations specified in the preceding section came from two major sources:

1. the inventory model for enlisted men

2. external sources.

The output of the inventory model for enlisted men which is used as input to the effectiveness model is discussed in Chapter 2 (in the section on relationships of the inventory model to other models).

The following data were obtained from sources external to the inventory model:

j is the coefficient in the quality factor $(Q(\rho))$

λ_k is the rate of technological change in an MOS

β_k is the desired career content ratio in an MOS

$a_{j(k)}$ is the relative proficiency rating of a first-year first-termer to that of a careerist in the kth MOS who was assigned to the jth class

$b_{j(k)}$ is the relative proficiency rating of a second-year first-termer to that of a careerist in the kth MOS who was assigned to the jth class

$c_{j(k)}$ is the relative proficiency rating of a third-year first-termer to that of a careerist in the kth MOS who was assigned to the jth class

TC_k is the training cost per man in an MOS.

The value 2 was assigned to j, a coefficient in the quality factor, and may overstate the adverse

effect on the effectiveness level during a major
buildup or phasedown. However, the purpose of assign-
ing such a high value was to stress the visible impact on the quality factor resulting from a dramatic
change in the trained base.

The rate of technological change for each MOS
(λ_k) was calculated to exceed somewhat the comparable
rates for the civilian economy, on the assumption that
military technology is changing at a faster rate than
civilian technology. For example, Solow's 1956 study[3]
and Kim's 1963 study[4] have estimated an overall λ for
the United States of about .015 (1.5 percent) per year.
For this study, the median value of λ_k was assumed to
be .03 (3 percent) per year, which is the same as
Solow's revised estimate (1960).[5] The upper and lower
limits on λ_k were specified as .09 and 0, respectively.

Given the lower, median, and upper values for λ_k,
the values for the 62 MOSs (except for MOS .09, which is
the training MOS) in Table 18 were obtained as follows:

1. The PEMA (Procurement of Equipment and
    Missiles, Army) component of training cost
    for each MOS was isolated, and the MOSs
    were then ranked in order of increasing
    PEMA cost.

2. The total training hours for each MOS were
    listed, and the MOSs were ranked in order
    of increasing hours.

3. The ranks for PEMA cost and training hours
    for each MOS were added together to obtain
    a composite rank. A final ranking was made
    on the basis of the composite rank.

4. The two median MOSs (ranks 31 and 32) were
    assigned the median ($\tilde{\lambda}$) of .03. For the 30
    MOSs ranking below the median, λ values were
    assigned varying from 0 to .029 at equal
    intervals of .001 ($= \frac{.03}{30}$), based on the
    final rank. For the 30 MOSs ranking above
    the median, λ values ranging from .032 to .09
    were assigned at equal intervals of .002
    ($= \frac{.06}{30}$), based on the final rank. In the case

of identical rankings, the interval was
split and the same λ value was assigned
to both MOS.

Thus, an ordinal value based on the PEMA cost and
training hours is used as a basis for the λ_k values.

The values of β_k (desired career content ratio
in each MOS) were obtained from an ODCSPER-SDY memorandum, "Enlisted Force Mix," dated July 12, 1967.
In order to make better use of the effectiveness
model, the values of both λ_k and β_k should be updated
periodically.

A relative proficiency rating of a first-termer
in the first, second, and third year of 22 selected
MOSs (numbered $j = 1,...,22$) is presented in Table
17. Each MOS (k) in Table 18 is assigned to a number
j in Table 17, and thus an assignment index j(k) was
obtained. The index j(k) is used as a subscript in
$a_{j(k)}$, $b_{j(k)}$, and $c_{j(k)}$, where a, b, and c are proficiency ratings for a first-year, a second-year,
and a third-year first-termer. For example, MOS 01
(Special Requirements) in Table 18 was assigned to
index 22 in Table 17. The assignment was made on
the basis of similarity between Department of Defense
occupational group classifications and Army Military
Occupational Specialty categories. Thus, the proficiency rating for assignment index 22 shows in
Table 17 that $a_{j(k)} = a_{22(01)} = 85\%$, $b_{j(k)} = b_{22(01)}$
$= 100\%$, and $c_{j(k)} = c_{22(01)} = 100\%$.

The training cost per man is calculated by add-
ing the following elements: OMA (Operations and
Maintenance, Army), MPA (Military Personnel, Army),
PEMA (Procurement of Equipment and Missiles, Army),
MCA (Military Construction, Army), and specialty pay.*

Data on costs were obtained from Gary Weinberg's
Army Training Cost Study (Draft TP, July, 1967),

------

*For convenience in calculations, specialty pay
was included in training costs. It was simply easier
to add it to training cost than to pay.

TABLE 17

Average Percentage Effectiveness of First-Termers
Relative to Fully Qualified Careerists by
Year of Service, Selected MOSs

	Percentage Effectiveness of First-Termer Relative to Fully Qualified Careerist			
	Year of Service			
MOS	1*	2	3	4
1. Linguist	30%	70%	90%	100%
2. Missile Repairman	31	59	87	100
3. Nuclear Powerman	32	55	81	100
4. Field Radio Repairman	34	69	94	100
5. Cryptanalytic Specialist	45	73	90	100
6. Aircraft Maintenance Mechanic	49	77	100	100
7. Intelligence Analyst	50	75	90	100
8. Track Vehicle Mechanic	51	85	100	100
9. Cartographic Draftsman	53	88	100	100
10. Air Defense Fire Control Crew	53	92	100	100
11. Field Communications Crew	54	88	100	100
12. Refrigeration Utilities Specialist	55	82	100	100
13. Personnel Specialist	58	91	100	100
14. Medical Specialist	60	85	100	100
15. Carpenter	65	87	100	100
16. Light Weapons Infantryman	65	90	100	100

Percentage Effectiveness of First-Termer
Relative to Fully Qualified Careerist

		Year of Service		
MOS	1*	2	3	4
17. Field Artillery Rocket Crew	65	89	100	100
18. Automotive Mechanic	67	94	100	100
19. Cook	70	95	100	100
20. Supply Handler	90	98	100	100
21. Driver	86	99	100	100
22. Scientific and Engineering Assistant	85	100	100	100

*Values in this column apply only to that portion of the first year of service during which the individual is in the operating forces. No allowance is made for training time here, during which the value will be definition by zero.

Source: Gorman C. Smith, Occupational Pay Differentials for Military Technicians, OASD, M&RA (1962), p. 134.

TABLE 18

Proficiency Index and Rate of Technological Change for Each MOS

Enlisted MOS Classification Structure	DOD[a] Occupational Group (2-Digit)	Assignment Index j(k) to Proficiency Rating by MOS[b]	PEMA Costs[c] Cost	PEMA Costs[c] Rank	Training Hours[c] Hours	Training Hours[c] Rank	Combined Total	Rank[d] Index	Rate of Technological Change (λ_k)[d]
0. Special Assignment									
00. Special Assignment (NEC)	43/50/51/83	22	15.58	56	50.98	58	114	57	.004
01. Special Requirements	44/50/54	22	0	0	0	0	0	0	.090
02. Bandsman	45	22	0		0	0	0	61	.000
03. Special Services	56	22	49.00	45	120.00	53	98	51	.010
04. Linguist	24	1	2172.24	1	1620.00	1	2	1	.088
05. Radio Code	20/28	7	283.43	15	355.85	23	38	18	.054
09. Reporting Codes (Training MOS)	56								
I. Tactical Operations									
11. Infantry-Armor	01/02/25	16	32.66	50	276.70	33	83	44	.017
12. Combat Engineering	03/25	11	26.13	52	127.75	51	103	52	.009
13. Field Cannon and Rocket Artillery	04/25	17	38.08	49	214.06	41	90	48	.013
15. Field Artillery Missiles	12/25	17	20.27	53	122.37	52	105	54	.007
16. Air Defense Missiles	12/25	10	115.81	27	316.48	29	56	26	.038
17. Combat Surveillance and Target Acquisition	03/22/41/60	11	87.58	32	235.67	38	70	34	.0265

Enlisted MOS Classification Structure	DOD[a] Occupational Group (2-Digit)	Assignment Index j(k) to Proficiency Rating by MOS[b]	PEMA Costs[c] Cost	Rank	Training Hours[c] Hours	Rank	Combined Total	Combined Rank[d] Index	Rate of Technological Change (λ_k)[d]
II. Missile and Fire Control Electronic Maintenance									
21. Ballistic Missile Electronic Maintenance	12/15	2	645.63	4	567.81	14	18	9	.071
22. Guided Missile Electronic Maintenance	12	2	456.07	9	911.33	5	14	7	.076
23. Missile Fire Control Electronic Maintenance	10/12	2	494.71	7	1385.78	2	9	4	.082
25. Fire Distribution Systems Repair	15	2	724.08	3	940.25	4	7	3	.084
26. Radar and Microwave Maintenance	10/19/22	4	522.82	6	842.24	6	12	5	.080
III. General Electronic Maintenance									
31. Field Communications Equipment Maintenance	10/16/19/20/58	4	322.60	13	653.87	9	22	11	.068
32. Fixed Plant Communications Equipment Maintenance	10/16	4	558.13	5	800.85	8	13	6	.078
33. Intercept Equipment Maintenance	10/19	4	422.87	10	807.00	7	17	8	.074
34. Data Processing Equipment Maintenance	11/13	2	927.32	2	1182.37	3	5	2	.086
35. Electrical/Electronic Devices Maintenance	10/14/19	4	371.81	12	404.92	21	33	15	.059
36. Wire Maintenance	62	5	45.69	46	138.43	50	96	50	.011

(cont.)

TABLE 18 (cont.)

Proficiency Index and Rate of Technological Change for Each MOS

Enlisted MOS Classification Structure	DOD[a] Occupational Group (2-Digit)	Assignment Index j(k) to Proficiency Rating by MOS[b]	PEMA Costs[c]		Training Hours[c]		Combined Rank[d]		Rate of Technological Change (λ_k)[d]
			Cost	Rank	Hours	Rank	Total	Index	
IV. Precision Maintenance									
41. Precision Devices	19/67/69	5	467.41	8	651.24	10	18	9	.071
42. Prosthetic Appliances	30/31/33	14	240.44	16	630.00	11	27	13	.064
43. Textile and Leather Repair	76/86	15	38.59	48	66.66	56	104	53	.008
44. Metalworking	70	15	207.02	18	267.37	35	53	25	.040
45. Armament Maintenance	63/64	8	237.45	17	333.41	25	42	22	.046
46. Missile Mechanical Maintenance	12/63	2	198.92	19	182.75	45	64	29	.032
V. Auxiliary Services									
51. Construction and Utilities	49/71/72/78/79	15	114.92	28	172.97	47	75	39	.0215
52. Power Production and Distribution	66/72	3	53.08	44	183.48	44	88	46	.0145
53. Industrial Gas Production	75	15	61.00	40	320.00	27	67	31	.029
54. Chemical	03/49/69	11	43.21	47	246.93	37	84	45	.016
55. Ammunition	43/64/82	8	111.14	30	253.00	36	66	30	.030
56. Supply Handling	82	20	12.53	59	64.52	57	116	58	.003
57. General Duty	49/76/84/83	22	.34	60	.87	60	120	60	.001

164

Enlisted MOS Classification Structure	DOD[a] Occupational Group (2-Digit)	Assignment Index j(k) to Proficiency Rating by MOS[b]	PEMA Costs[c] Cost	Rank	Training Hours[c] Hours	Rank	Combined Rank[d] Total	Index	Rate of Technological Change (λk)[d]
VI. Motors									
61. Marine Operations	65/81	13	58.62	42	173.09	46	88	46	.0145
62. Engineer Heavy Equipment Operations and Maintenance	61/63/73	15	65.21	39	185.26	43	82	42	.0185
63. Automotive Maintenance	61/69	18	84.74	33	268.19	34	67	31	.029
64. Motor Transit	81	21	18.63	54	80.34	54	108	55	.006
65. Railway Maintenance	66/69	8	169.38	23	440.00	18	41	20	.049
66. Railway Operations	81	8	169.38	23	440.00	18	41	20	.049
67. Aircraft Maintenance	60	6	56.74	43	150.45	49	92	49	.012
68. Aircraft Components Repair	60	6	123.29	26	322.39	26	52	24	.042
VII. Clerical									
70. Clerk	24/50/51/56/57	13	80.26	35	320.00	27	62	27	.036
71. Administration	24/50/51/56/57	13	78.42	36	227.83	39	75	39	.0215
72. Communications Center Operations	58	11	28.16	51	431.27	20	71	36	.0245
73. Finance	54	13	14.74	58	34.34	59	117	59	.002
74. Data Processing	53	9	81.96	34	171.56	48	82	42	.0185
76. Supply	40/55	18	74.21	38	278.55	32	70	34	.0265
VIII. Graphics									
81. Drafting Cartography	41/81	9	106.33	31	227.59	40	71	36	.0245
82. Surveying	41	9	60.71	41	298.72	31	72	38	.023
83. Printing	74	15	187.05	21	209.94	42	63	28	.034
84. Pictorial	19/40	9	304.53	14	492.34	16	30	14	.062

(cont.)

TABLE 18 (cont.)

Proficiency Index and Rate of Technological Change for Each MOS

Enlisted MOS Classification Structure	DOD[a] Occupational Group (2-Digit)	Assignment Index j(1) to Proficiency Rating by MOS[b]	PEMA Costs[c] Cost	Rank	Training Hours[c] Hours	Rank	Combined Rank[c] Total	Index	Rate of Technological Change (λ_k)[d]
IX. General Technical									
91. Medical Care and Treatment	30/31/37/33	14	172.90	22	478.00	17	39	19	.052
92. Laboratory Procedures	31/49	14	18.59	55	73.21	55	110	56	.005
93. Technical Equipment Operations	19/22/23/42	5	418.71	11	548.96	15	26	12	.066
94. Food Service	80	19	77.52	37	306.31	30	67	31	.029
95. Law Enforcement	16/83	16	15.14	57	346.27	24	81	41	.020
96. General Intelligence	24	7	111.20	29	375.91	22	51	23	.044
97. Special Intelligence	24	7	144.09	25	616.72	12	37	17	.056
98. Signal Intelligence	7/23	7	192.60	20	587.00	13	33	15	.059

[a] From OASD, Occupational Conversion Table: Enlisted, DOD 1312.1-E DA PAM 611-12 (March, 1967).

[b] Index for each MOS is derived by comparing two-digit occupational group with that of MOS in Table 17. The index runs from 1 to 22.

[c] Abstracted from the data section in Gary Weinberg's Army Training Cost Study (Draft TP, July, 1967), Project 007.106, Economic and Costing Department, Research Analysis Corporation. Weinberg's data, which have five-digit MOS detail, were aggregated to three-digit detail by simple averaging. This, in turn, was aggregated to two-digit detail by using weighted averages, the weight being the proportions of three-digit MOS in a two-digit MOS. The weights used were obtained from an ODCSPER-SDY memorandum entitled "Enlisted Force Mix" (July 12, 1967).

[d] See the text in this section.

166

Project 007.106, Economics and Costing Department, Research Analysis Corporation. The following comments are made concerning this data:

1. It applies only to specialized training for enlisted men beyond basic combat training (BCT). It includes all advanced individual training (AIT), whether taught at CONARC (Continental Army Command) service schools or training centers, and excludes BCT costs and costs of on-the-job training.

2. It includes a discussion of current data base, specific data requirements, and additional new cost data to be developed.

3. Cost items included are the following:

    a. Transportation costs (to and from training establishments for both students and faculty)

    b. Housing, food, medical, and recreational costs (for both students and faculty)

    c. Pay for both students and faculty

    d. Maintenance costs of the training facility

    e. Purchase costs, maintenance costs, and overhaul costs of training equipment

    f. Training aids

    g. Others.

4. The costs applicable to training are those budget appropriations described in AR-37-100, the Army Management Structure (AMS)-Fiscal Code.

5. The cost data have five-digit MOS details
    and are expressed in fiscal 1966 dollars.

In order to utilize Weinberg's data, it was
necessary to make the following calculations:

1. Five-digit MOS detail was aggregated to
    three-digit detail by simple averaging.

2. Three-digit MOS detail, obtained from the
    above step, was aggregated to two-digit
    detail by using weighted averages, the
    weight being the proportions of three-digit
    MOS in a two-digit MOS. The weights used
    were obtained from an ODCSPER-SDY memoran-
    dum entitled "Enlisted Force Mix" (July 12,
    1967).

The actual data used in this study for calculation of the total training cost for each enlisted
man do not include the cost of basic combat training
and on-the-job training in the final results. It is
believed that the cost of basic training per enlisted
man was, on the average, $500 in fiscal 1967.

RESULTS AND INTERPRETATIONS

The results from the equations listed in Table 16
are calculated by the computer. Detailed extracts of
the printout are not reproduced here. However, Table
19 presents, in summary form, some cost calculations
performed by the model.

Pay is estimated by use of the fiscal 1970 pay
table; training cost is expressed in 1967 dollars.
The number of enlisted men and its composition (by
grade, year of service, and other characteristics)
are taken from the results of the inventory model
of enlisted men.

TABLE 19

Total Costs of Pay and Training for Enlisted Men

Fiscal Year	Pay[a] (in thousands)	Pay plus training costs[b] (in thousands)
1969	$4,044,558	$4,963,424
1970	3,822,194	4,748,152
1971	3,681,778	4,598,271
1972	3,653,853	4,569,397
1973	3,629,322	4,544,828
1974	3,599,903	4,515,409
1975	3,575,987	4,491,494
1976	3,565,946	4,481,452
1977	3,551,879	4,467,385
1978	3,550,773	4,466,279
1979	3,545,142	4,460,649
1980	3,545,875	4,461,382

[a]Includes basic pay, subsistence and quarters allowances, and tax advantage.

[b]Training costs exclude the cost of basic combat training (BCT). In order to estimate total training costs including the cost of BCT, total accessions multiplied by the fixed cost of BCT per man must be added to this column.

Source: Summary of cost calculations performed by the Cost and Relative Effectiveness Model.

170 THE ALL-VOLUNTEER ARMY

NOTES

1. K. H. Kim et al., An Army 75 Personnel Procurement Concept (Battelle Memorial Institute, July 31, 1968). For the Department of the Army, Contract DAHC 19 67 C 0031.

2. See "Cost/Effectiveness of Reenlistment Incentives," Appendix to Annex G, Navy Manpower Considerations, 1970-1980, Study 13, Institute of Naval Studies (February, 1966).

3. Robert M. Solow, "Technical Change and the Aggregate Production Function," Review of Economics and Statistics (1957), Vol. 39, No. 3, 312-20.

4. K. H. Kim, "An Econometric Growth Model of the U.S., 1902-52, With Emphasis on Monetary Controls" (unpublished paper, 1963).

5. Robert M. Solow, "Investment and Technical Progress," Mathematical Methods in the Social Sciences: Proceedings of the First Stanford Symposium, Stanford Mathematical Studies in the Social Sciences, IV (Stanford: Stanford University Press, 1960), pp. 89-104.

CHAPTER **6** COST ESTIMATE MODELS
FOR OFFICERS AND
WARRANT OFFICERS

OFFICERS

Costs for officers are estimated in two parts:
pay and allowances, and procurement and training
costs. Details of the data on allowances, including
information on the distribution of marital and dependency status (on which pay partly depends), are explained in the discussion of the inventory model in
Chapter 2. Procurement and training costs are explained in this chapter. Excerpts from the computer
printout of this model do not appear in this book.

Description of Calculations

The model makes five sets of cost calculations.
The first set is for total pay and allowances paid
to the inventory of officers in each branch; the
second is for total procurement and training costs
for the accessions in each branch; the third is the
sum of the first two sets of costs for each branch.
The fourth and fifth are the sum of the pay and allowances (calculated in the first set) over all
branches and the sum of the procurement and training
costs (calculated in the second set) over all branches.

In deriving total training costs for enlisted
men (in Chapter 2), training cost per enlisted man
by MOS was multiplied by the number of men in the MOS
rather than by the number of accessions; the total
training cost was then added to the total of pay and
allowances in the same MOS. Thus, the total cost for
the number of enlisted men in each MOS was derived.
This procedure for calculating total cost for enlisted

men is based on the assumption that every man in a
given MOS incurs a certain amount of training at
some point in his Army career. This is also true in
the case of officers. However, training costs for
officers also vary by the source of the commission.
In order to estimate annual training costs for a
given inventory, it would be helpful to know the ex-
act proportion of officers from each source already
in the inventory at the beginning of the simulation
period. The officer inventory model, however, does
not distinguish each officer by the source of his
commission. Therefore, unlike the cost estimates
for enlisted men, total officer costs are based on
the pay and allowances of the inventory and the procurement and training costs for the accessions. Because of this, the total cost figures underestimate
total training costs by the amount incurred for training officers who were in the inventory prior to the
beginning of the simulation period.

The following assumptions were made in calculating procurement and training costs:

1. A fixed number of accessions will come from
    the United States Military Academy (USMA)
    each year from fiscal 1969 to 1980, as
    shown below.

Fiscal Year	Number of Accessions
1969	600
1970	700
1971	800
1972	900
1973	900
1974	900
1975	900
1976	900
1977	900
1978	900
1979	900
1980	900

2. The distribution of USMA and Officer Candi-
    date School (OCS) officers among the first

14 Army Promotion List (APL) officer
branches is fixed in the proportions
shown below. Graduates of USMA, although concentrated in five arms (Infantry, Armor, Artillery, Signal Corps,
and Corps of Engineers), are commissioned in the first 14 APL branches.
Each of these branches is given a pro-
portionate share of USMA graduates based
on the total number of officers authorized in that branch. Normally those USMA
officers commissioned in other than the
five arms mentioned above are required to
serve a one-year tour with one of the
three combat arms (Infantry, Artillery,
and Armor); in some cases, however, they
are excluded from this detail because of
inability to meet physical standards.
In this study, the number and proportions
commissioned in branches other than the
five arms are ignored because the proportion of USMA graduates assigned to each of
the other branches is almost insignificant:
they total about 5 percent of the whole.

An ROTC (Reserve Officer Training
Corps) graduate, on the other hand, may be
commissioned in any one of 15 basic branches:
Infantry, Armor, Field Artillery, Air De-
fense, Signal Corps, Corps of Engineers,
Adjutant General's Corps, Military Intel-
ligence, Chemical Corps, Finance Corps,
Military Police Corps, Ordnance Corps,
Quartermaster Corps, Transportation Corps,
and Medical Service Corps.

There are only three OCSs--Infantry, Artillery, and Engineer--in operation at the
present time, and the number is subject to
change. Furthermore, because of differences in orientation, curricula, selection
criteria, and cost, graduates from the OCS
for Infantry are assigned only to Infantry,
those from the OCS for Artillery only to
Artillery, etc. It is believed that during

peacetime these three schools will continue in operation.

TABLE 20

Distribution of USMA and OCS Officers Over First
14 APL Officer Branches, June 30, 1967

Branch (k) Number and Branch Name	Proportion of USMA Officers in Branch	Proportion of OCS Officers in Branch
1. Infantry	.30	.4465
2. Field Artillery	.25	.2526
3. Air Defense	.09	.0978
4. Armor	.15	
5. Chemical	.00	
6. Engineer	.11	.2031
7. Ordnance	.00	
8. Quartermaster	.00	
9. Signal	.10	
10. Transportation	.00	
11. Adjutant General	.00	
12. Finance	.00	
13. Military Police	.00	
14. Military Intelligence	.00	
	1.00	1.0000

Source: Figures based on "FY Gains to Date,
June 30, 1967," OPO (August 16, 1967).

3. The number of accessions specified by the
    inventory model as necessary for branches
    15 through 22 are simply assigned to them.
    Personnel in any of these branches cannot
    be assigned to any other branch. Branches
    15 through 22 are Women's Army Corps, Chap-
    lain, Judge Advocate General, Medical Corps,
    Dental Corps, Medical Service Corps, Veter-
    inarians Corps, and Army Nurse Corps.

4. The number of accessions from USMA in each
    branch (as specified by Assumptions 1 and
    2) is subtracted from annual accessions
    required for each branch (calculated in
    the officer inventory model). The resid-
    uals in all branches are added and the
    sum of accessions still required thus de-
    rived is distributed between OCS and ROTC
    officers in the following proportions:
    ROTC .88; OCS .12. The estimated number
    of officer accessions from OCS obtained in
    this manner is then distributed (according
    to the proportions specified in Assumption
    2) among those branches in which vacancies
    remain after accessions from USMA are dis-
    tributed. If there is no vacancy in a
    branch, no accession is brought from OCS.
    Any vacancies which remain after all USMA
    and OCS officers have been distributed are
    filled with ROTC officers.

5. The precommissioning cost for non-APL
    branches is assumed to be zero.

Data on Procurement and Training Costs

Data on the procurement and training cost per
officer by source-branch is supplied externally. It
varies from one source-branch to another because of
different costs associated with source and branch.
It also varies according to the level of procurement
due to changes in the cost of construction (MCA cost)
for OCSs. Clearly, the average (or total) cost of
procurement and training is a function of the level
of officer production. The fixed cost for each
source-branch used in this study is generally not
acceptable when accessions fluctuate widely. However,
in the absence of a meaningful cost function, this
study assigns all costs to a set of fixed values.

Some explanation is needed for the cost data
provided in Table 21. The first point requiring explanation is the MCA cost per student. Institutions
such as USMA and the universities and colleges

offering the ROTC program do not require a special
capital budget when the number of students enrolled
changes. Even if such a budget were required, the
long periods over which such institutions operate
make the capital cost per student very small. In
the case of the OCSs, however, the periods of operation are generally intermittent. They are opened
and closed according to the needs of the Army, and
the costs associated with such a flexible program
are a major consideration (aside from factors of
quality) in personnel procurement from this source.
There are two major difficulties in assessing the
capital cost of each OCS student. The first is estimation of the precise number of OCS students who
will be produced by an undetermined number of schools
over an undetermined period of time in which the
schools will be required. The second is estimation
of a reasonably correct capital cost for each OCS
school. In most cases, it is almost impossible to
separate the capital costs of OCS activities from
those of other activities because the schools are
located with other Army activities and are integrated
from an operational standpoint. Regardless of how
student production and capital costs are estimated,
it is necessary to treat the capital cost of an OCS
as a short-run (or variable) cost item. In general,
the capital cost of a school was divided by the number of OCS graduates produced during the period.

The second cost item which may require some explanation is the cost of the Ranger training course,
which is technically mandatory for all newly commissioned Regular Army (RA) lieutenants regardless of the
source of their commission. As of June, 1968, however,
only five officer branches (Infantry, Artillery, Armor, Engineer, and Signal) were actually taking the
Ranger training course. The Army anticipates return-
ing to the mandatory policy after conclusion of the
war in Southeast Asia. For purposes of this study,
however, it was assumed that all newly commissioned
USMA officers, distinguished military graduates (DMG)
of ROTC and OCS officers are taking Ranger training.

The data used in calculating the total cost of
officer training is summarized in Table 21.

TABLE 21

Average Training Costs per Officer, by Source and Branch[a]

	Precommissioning Cost	Construction (MCA) Cost	Cost of Ranger Training
USMA	$13,475	Nominal	$4,408
ROTC	6,541	Nominal	441[b]
OCS--Infantry	11,393	$ 3,282	4,408
Artillery	12,068	4,183	4,408
Armor	9,033	8,780	4,408
Engineer	7,224	1,687	4,408
Ordnance	8,671	13,043	4,408
Quartermaster	6,383	1,615	4,408
Signal	9,705	473	4,408
Transportation	8,112	5,675	4,408
Women's Army Corps (Branch 15)	11,393[c]	3,282[c]	0

Cost of Basic Branch Qualification

Branch No.	Branch	
1	Infantry	$2,091
2	Field Artillery	3,407
3	Air Defense	3,407
4	Armor	4,391
5	Chemical	2,575
6	Engineer	1,998
7	Ordnance	1,400
8	Quartermaster	1,749
9	Signal	2,286
10	Transportation	3,656
11	Adjutant General	1,319
12	Finance	1,742
13	Military Police	2,410
14	Military Intelligence	1,555
15	Women's Army Corps	2,091
16	Chaplain	3,897
17	Judge Advocate	0
18	Medical	940
19	Dental	940
20	Veterinary	940
21	Medical Service	1,270
22	Army Nurse	1,270

[a]Reflecting fiscal 1966 costs.

[b]Ten percent of $4,408 is used because, on the average, distinguished military graduates (DMG) of ROTC are 10 percent of total ROTC graduates. The DMG are the only graduates of ROTC who take Ranger training.

[c]Precommissioning and construction (MCA) costs for the Women's Army Corps were assumed to be the same as those for OCS--Infantry.

Source: K. H. Kim et al., An Army 75 Personnel Procurement Concept (Battelle Memorial Institute, July 31, 1968). For the Department of the Army, Contract DAHC 19 67 C 0031.

WARRANT OFFICERS

Description of Calculations

The cost calculations for the pay and allowances
of warrant officers are identical with those for officers, but the calculations for training costs dif-
fer. As mentioned in Chapter 2, the inventory data
on years of service for warrant officers are by years
of "active federal service" rather than years of "active federal commissioned service." Furthermore, a
significantly large number of warrant officers have
active service experience prior to their being commissioned as warrant officers, and most of them come
from the ranks of enlisted men. Therefore, in the
calculation of training costs, the cost of their pay
and allowances as enlisted men is included as a precommissioning cost. Consequently, underestimating
of salaries and allowances in the total cost estimate
is avoided. However, the cost estimate for the Army
as a whole may suffer from double-counting, since pay
and allowances for enlisted men are already included
in the cost estimates for enlisted men.

Data on Replacement Costs

The best data available on warrant officer training costs is data published by the Department of the
Army on the estimated costs of replacing warrant officers, by branch. The elements of cost included in
these estimates are salaries and allowances (MPA) and
operations and maintenance (O&MA); they do not include construction (MCA) or equipment (PEMA) costs.

The data used were "Estimated Cost of Replacing
U.S. Army Warrant Officers," by MOS, Fiscal 1966
(these costs are detailed by four-digit MOS) and
"Actual Warrant Officer Strength" as of June 30, 1967
(by branch and four-digit MOS).

Calculation of Average Replacement Costs

The data described above were used to calculate
average replacement cost per warrant officer, by
branch, as follows:

APPENDIXES

APPENDIX A

Sample Computer Printouts from Civilian
Manpower Pool Model

AVAILABLE WHITE CIVILIAN MALE MANPOWER IN THE UNITED STATES, 1972
INCLUDING 1-Y, 4-F, AND TAKEOUTS

	TOTAL	16 YEARS OF AGE	17 YEARS OF AGE	18 YEARS OF AGE	19 YEARS OF AGE	20 YEARS OF AGE	21 YEARS OF AGE	22 YEARS OF AGE	23 YEARS OF AGE	24 YEARS OF AGE	25 YEARS OF AGE	26 YEARS OF AGE
GRAND TOTAL	17820981	1767395	1760996	1717996	1688995	1640397	1592799	1551799	1570799	1584336	1729826	1215644
MARRIED WITH DEPENDENTS	3653223	3229	12253	25375	74463	181268	235490	506783	628494	694438	759140	532321
MARRIED WITHOUT DEPENDENTS	2226667	5128	17567	38590	114316	178863	237777	267777	330647	362711	393716	279574
SINGLE	11941091	1759038	1731175	1654031	1500217	1280265	1119560	777240	611659	527187	576969	403750
GRAND TOTAL	17820981	1767395	1760996	1717996	1688995	1640397	1592799	1551799	1570799	1584336	1729826	1215644
ENROLLED BELOW COLLEGE	3675157	1682953	1410566	358273	101897	23238	5532	19770	7085	23126	24631	18085
ENROLLED IN COLLEGE	4368509	5534	144966	770573	933178	886208	687016	319459	220427	140689	151156	109302
ENROLLED GRADUATE	554403	0	0	0	-110	6661	37401	138308	108573	92595	98736	72239
NOT ENROLLED NON HIGH GRAD	2411087	75058	166990	233007	173979	212852	216351	262038	276545	276125	312166	205975
NOT ENROLLED HIGH SCHOOL GRAD	6811825	3849	38473	356142	480051	511938	646499	812224	958169	1051801	1142936	810043
MARRIED WITH DEPENDENTS	3653223	3229	12253	25375	74463	181268	235460	506783	628494	694438	759140	532321
ENROLLED BELOW COLLEGE	31393	392	1080	2058	7302	1720	1787	2747	3444	3810	4092	2961
ENROLLED IN COLLEGE	319008	242	1647	3918	11637	32197	44564	37510	45458	49769	53314	38753
ENROLLED GRADUATE	97690	0	0	0	0	550	735	16216	19527	21312	22665	16686
NOT ENROLLED NON HIGH GRAD	904108	2265	4641	9983	28644	53127	64949	115641	148240	165928	186096	124595
NOT ENROLLED HIGH SCHOOL GRAD	2301024	331	4886	9416	26880	93073	123426	334670	411825	453618	492973	349326
MARRIED WITHOUT DEPENDENTS	2226667	5128	17567	38590	114316	178863	237779	267777	330647	362711	393716	279574
ENROLLED BELOW COLLEGE	28606	657	1763	3864	12560	1338	1442	1053	1409	1580	1775	1185
ENROLLED IN COLLEGE	392301	406	3205	7623	22613	53711	74720	38387	46531	50918	54434	39654
ENROLLED GRADUATE	147595	0	0	0	0	1947	2715	23668	29892	31362	33582	24428
NOT ENROLLED NON HIGH GRAD	356646	3276	4955	11641	33880	32012	39721	36253	46277	51704	57795	38931
NOT ENROLLED HIGH SCHOOL GRAD	1301719	789	7643	15483	45263	89855	119181	168415	206538	227146	246031	175375
SINGLE	11941091	1759038	1731175	1654031	1500217	1280265	1119560	777240	611659	527187	576969	403750
ENROLLED BELOW COLLEGE	3615157	1681904	1407724	352372	82035	20179	2304	15970	2232	17735	18764	13938
ENROLLED IN COLLEGE	3657200	4887	140115	759032	898928	800300	567732	243563	128439	40002	43307	30895
ENROLLED GRADUATE	309119	0	0	0	-110	3963	33951	98425	59154	39921	42690	31126
NOT ENROLLED NON HIGH GRAD	1150533	69518	157394	211384	111456	127713	111681	110144	82028	58493	68275	42448
NOT ENROLLED HIGH SCHOOL GRAD	3209082	2729	25943	331243	407908	328111	403892	309138	339806	371037	403933	285342

187

AVAILABLE NONWHITE CIVILIAN MALE MANPOWER IN THE UNITED STATES, 1972
INCLUDING 1-Y, 4-F, AND TAKEOUTS

	TOTAL	16 YEARS OF AGE	17 YEARS OF AGE	18 YEARS OF AGE	19 YEARS OF AGE	20 YEARS OF AGE	21 YEARS OF AGE	22 YEARS OF AGE	23 YEARS OF AGE	24 YEARS OF AGE	25 YEARS OF AGE	26 YEARS OF AGE
GRAND TOTAL	2670522	287600	283600	271600	264600	246198	245796	238795	230795	220336	177174	204029
MARRIED WITH DEPENDENTS	583621	378	1107	4535	14978	32804	51668	102779	101635	100267	80626	92846
MARRIED WITHOUT DEPENDENTS	264334	267	804	3759	12173	19619	30862	42204	41814	41329	33233	38270
SINGLE	1822567	286954	281689	263306	237448	193775	163266	93813	87347	78740	63316	72913
GRAND TOTAL	2670522	287600	283600	271600	264600	246198	245796	238795	230795	220336	177174	204029
ENROLLED BELOW COLLEGE	66173	268685	225326	113964	36920	8000	3172	5022	3003	770	619	713
ENROLLED IN COLLEGE	341243	577	21748	53182	81756	78646	41213	25716	11500	9855	7924	9125
ENROLLED GRADUATE	24550	0	0	0	110	558	1588	6119	4385	4319	3473	3999
NOT ENROLLED NON HIGH GRAD	728712	17950	29303	56938	54790	67720	99421	94637	87634	80700	64892	74728
NOT ENROLLED HIGH SCHOOL GRAD	909844	387	7224	47535	91024	91274	100402	107301	124275	124692	100266	115464
MARRIED WITH DEPENDENTS	583621	378	1107	4535	14978	32804	51668	102779	101635	100267	80626	92846
ENROLLED BELOW COLLEGE	5888	147	284	1129	2184	281	519	336	295	261	210	242
ENROLLED IN COLLEGE	17280	12	78	123	207	1210	2057	2897	2883	2862	2301	2650
ENROLLED GRADUATE	2957	0	0	0		89	151	581	576	572	460	529
NOT ENROLLED NON HIGH GRAD	253797	213	525	1664	6535	16030	25081	44698	43378	42596	34252	39444
NOT ENROLLED HIGH SCHOOL GRAD	303699	5	220	1619	6052	15194	23880	54867	54502	53976	43403	49981
MARRIED WITHOUT DEPENDENTS	264334	267	804	3759	12173	19619	30862	42204	41814	41329	33233	38270
ENROLLED BELOW COLLEGE	4888	88	201	797	1278	179	324	456	433	414	333	384
ENROLLED IN COLLEGE	17572	12	93	149	258	1301	2061	2916	2905	2885	2320	2672
ENROLLED GRADUATE	8303	0	0	0		5	5	1762	1758	1748	1406	1619
NOT ENROLLED NON HIGH GRAD	86115	165	398	1497	5730	7215	11295	12938	12731	12507	10057	11581
NOT ENROLLED HIGH SCHOOL GRAD	147457	3	111	1316	4908	10919	17176	24132	23986	23774	19117	22015
SINGLE	1822567	286954	281689	263306	237448	193775	163266	93813	87347	78740	63316	72913
ENROLLED BELOW COLLEGE	655398	268450	224841	112018	33458	7541	2329	4230	2274	94	76	87
ENROLLED IN COLLEGE	306390	553	21577	52910	81291	76135	37095	19903	5712	4108	3303	3804
ENROLLED GRADUATE	13291	0	0	0	110	464	1432	3776	2051	1999	1608	1852
NOT ENROLLED NON HIGH GRAD	388600	17572	28379	53777	42524	44475	63065	37602	31525	25597	20583	23702
NOT ENROLLED HIGH SCHOOL GRAD	458688	379	6893	44600	80065	65161	59346	28302	45786	46942	37747	43468

APPENDIX B

Definitions and Data Used in Chapter 4

ENLISTEES IN MENTAL CATEGORY IV AS PROPORTION
OF TOTAL ENLISTMENT, 1959-69

Calendar Year		Total Number of Enlistees	Number of Enlistees in Mental Category IV	Proportion of Enlistees in Mental Category IV
1959	DOD	271,234	13,238	.0488
	Army	90,932	0	.0000
1960	DOD	330,914	32,105	.0970
	Army	100,498	0	.0000
1961	DOD	352,485	22,191	.0630
	Army	117,824	0	.0000
1962	DOD	324,256	23,234	.0717
	Army	109,938	4,789	.0436
1963	DOD	306,584	25,013	.0816
	Army	100,737	7,194	.0714
1964	DOD	304,965	20,540	.0674
	Army	106,946	7,688	.0719
1965	DOD	385,827	39,027	.1012
	Army	115,852	12,436	.1073
1966	DOD	550,682	71,135	.1292
	Army	202,363	43,087	.2129
1967	DOD	433,020	88,612	.2046
	Army	171,183	43,502	.2541
1968	DOD	516,625	109,116	.2112
	Army	199,532	49,360	.2474
1969[a]	DOD	125,955	30,366	.2411
	Army	45,458	13,297	.2925

[a]Data cover the first quarter only.

Source: Abstracted from annual and monthly reports of the qualitative distribution of military manpower program.

DEFINITIONS OF VARIABLES FOR REGRESSION ANALYSIS
OF TIME-SERIES ON ENLISTMENTS

E_1 is the number of men in mental categories I-III who enlisted in the Army during the specified calendar quarter.

E_2 is the number of men in mental categories I-III who enlisted in all the services during the specified calendar quarter.

P_1 is the average number of Selective Service registrants aged 19-26 in the 50 states and the District of Columbia whose classification status was 1A or 1AO over the specified calendar quarter.

P_2 is the average number of Selective Service registrants in the 50 states and the District of Columbia over the specified calendar quarter, excluding 1A and 1AO registrants aged 26 and over and all registrants whose classification status was 1Y, 4F, 1C, 4A, or 5A.

W_c is the median earnings which, during a specified calendar quarter, a year-round, full-time, 18-year-old civilian male worker can anticipate receiving over the next three years.

W_{m1} is the military earnings which can be anticipated by a young man who enlists in the Army for a three-year period during the specified calendar quarter (includes basic pay, quarters allowance, subsistence allowance, imputed value of medical services).

W_{m2} is the military earnings which can be anticipated by a young man who enlists in the armed forces for a three-year period during the specified calendar quarter (includes basic pay, quarters allowance, subsistence allowance, imputed value of medical services).

U_1 is the unemployment rate of male workers aged 16-19 during the specified calendar quarter.

U_2 is the unemployment rate of male workers aged 16-21 whose "major activity" was other than attending school during the specified calendar quarter.

U_3 is the unemployment rate of male workers aged 18-19 during the specified calendar quarter.

A_1 is the total number of accessions (enlistments plus inductions) to the Army during the specified calendar quarter.

A_2 is the total number of accessions (enlistments plus inductions) to all the services during the specified calendar quarter.

D_1 is a dummy variable (1 for the first calendar quarter of the year, 0 for the other quarters).

D_2 is a dummy variable (1 for the second calendar quarter of the year, 0 for the other quarters).

D_3 is a dummy variable (1 for the third calendar quarter of the year, 0 for the other quarters).

MANIPULATION OF RAW DATA TO OBTAIN VARIABLES
FOR REGRESSION ANALYSIS OF TIME-SERIES
ON ENLISTMENTS

E_1 For the period beginning with the third quarter
of 1958 and ending with the third quarter of
1963, it was assumed that all inductions were to
the Army. (Actually, during this period there
were never more than 100 inductions per fiscal
year to all the other services combined.) On
this assumption, the number of inductees per
quarter in mental categories I-III was subtracted
from the total number of chargeable male accessions to the Army in mental categories I-III per
quarter. This number was considered to be the
number of young men in mental categories I-III
who enlisted in the Army during a specified
quarter.

Beginning with the fourth quarter of 1963,
when monthly reports of qualitative distribution
became available, the monthly totals of Army enlistees in mental categories I-III are added in
three-month clusters to obtain the number in
mental categories I-III who enlisted in the
Army per quarter.

E_2 For the period beginning with the third quarter
of 1958 and ending with the third quarter of
1963, the number of Army enlistees per quarter
in mental categories I-III (obtained as explained
above) was added to the number of chargeable
male accessions to all the other services in mental categories I-III per quarter. This procedure assumes that all accessions to services
other than the Army are enlistments--a corollary
to the assumption on which E_1 for this time
period is based.

Beginning with the fourth quarter of 1963,
monthly totals of enlistees in mental categories
I-III for each of the services are added in
three-month clusters to obtain the total number
of young men in mental categories I-III who

enlisted in the armed services during a specified quarter.

P$_1$ The number of Selective Service registrants classified 1A or 1AO as of March 31, June 30, September 30, and December 31 of each year was drawn from monthly reports of the Selective Service system. The number for each of these months was adjusted by subtracting the total number of 1A and 1AO registrants in the Canal Zone, Guam, Puerto Rico, and the Virgin Islands as of June 30 of the appropriate year, as recorded in the Annual Report of the Director of Selective Service. The result of this step was assumed to be the total number of registrants classified 1A and 1AO in the 50 states and the District of Columbia as of the end of March, June, September, or December of each year.

In a separate step, the number of registrants classified 1A or 1AO who were aged 26 and over or under 19 as of March 31, June 30, September 30, and December 31 of each year was drawn from the monthly Selective Service reports. The number for each of these months was adjusted by subtracting the number of 1A and 1AO registrants in the Canal Zone, Guam, Puerto Rico, and the Virgin Islands who were 26 and over or under 19 as of June 30 of the appropriate year, as recorded in the Annual Report of the Director of Selective Service.

This number was then subtracted from the total number of 1A and 1AO registrants in the 50 states and the District of Columbia, to obtain the number of 1A and 1AO registrants aged 19-26 as of the end of March, June, September, or December of each year (in the 50 states and the District of Columbia).

The number of 1A and 1AO registrants aged 19-26 actually used in the regression for each quarter is an average of the number as of the end of the month ending that quarter and the number as of the end of the month ending the preceding quarter.

195

P_2 The total number of classified Selective Service registrants as of March 31, June 30, September 30, and December 31 of each year was drawn from monthly reports of the Selective Service system. The number for each of these months was reduced by the number of 1A and 1AO registrants aged 26 and over plus all registrants whose classification status was 1Y, 4F, 1C, 4A, or 5A, according to these same monthly reports.

     The results of this procedure were adjusted by subtracting the number of 1A and 1AO registrants in the Canal Zone, Guam, Puerto Rico, and the Virgin Islands who were 26 and over plus all registrants in these areas whose classification status was 1Y, 4F, 1C, 4A, or 5A as of June 30 of the appropriate year, as recorded in the Annual Report of the Director of Selective Service.

     The number thus obtained is the total number of Selective Service registrants in the 50 states and the District of Columbia as of the end of March, June, September, or December of each year--excluding registrants who are classified 1A or 1AO but are 26 and over; who have completed their military service; who are physically, mentally, or morally unfit; who are qualified for military service only in time of war or national emergency; who are over the age of liability for military service; or who are serving in the armed forces. It is assumed to be the total number of Selective Service registrants available and qualified for military service during the specified quarter.

     The number actually used in the regression for each quarter is an average of the number as of the end of the month ending that quarter and the number as of the end of the month ending the preceding quarter.

W_c The median annual income of year-round, full-time male workers aged 14-19 and 20-24 was obtained for each year from 1958 to 1968 from the Bureau of the Census. These income figures were

assumed to represent median earnings, since for
the age groups in question the median income of
year-round, full-time workers probably includes
relatively little income from sources other than
earnings. In addition, since most 14-16-year-
olds are enrolled in school, it was assumed that
the incomes of 17-19-year-olds dominate the reported figures.

Since the typical enlistee is 18 years old,
it can be said that he forgoes two years of civilian income at the median level for 14-19-year-
olds and one year of income at the median level
for 20-24-year-olds over the three-year period
of his enlistment. On this assumption, the following calculation was performed for each year
from 1958 to 1968:

3 (2/3 [median income of 14-19-year-olds]
+ 1/3 [median income of 20-24-year-olds])

The amount calculated for each year was then adjusted by the consumer price index for that year.

Since the survey on which the Census Bureau
figures are based is taken in the third quarter
of each year, the amount obtained for each year
by performing the calculations described above
was assumed to be the income forgone by enlistment in the third quarter. An estimate of the income forgone by enlistment in the intervening quarters of each year was obtained by interpolation.

The result obtained by this procedure is
assumed to be the median earnings which, during
a specified calendar quarter, a year-round, full-
time, 18 year-old civilian male worker can anticipate receiving over the next three years.

W_{m1} From an unpublished paper prepared for a Department of Defense pay study group in 1962, it was
determined that 84.95 percent of cash pay to enlisted men in general is composed of basic pay,
quarters allowance, and subsistence allowance
(as of fiscal 1961). In addition, it was

determined that the value of medical services
received by enlisted men in general is 3.22 percent of cash pay (as of fiscal 1961). On the
basis of these figures plus the amounts actually
paid to an enlisted man in basic pay and quarters and subsistence allowances in fiscal 1961,
it was possible to establish the value of medical services received by an average enlisted man
as approximately $253 annually.

In a separate step, Department of Defense
pay schedules were consulted to determine the
amount of money paid to Army enlisted men in
grades E-1, E-2, E-3, E-4 for basic pay and
quarters and subsistence allowances during each
year from 1958 to 1969. The total paid to a
man enlisting in the Army during a specified
calendar quarter over the entire period of his
first enlistment was then calculated on the
basis of the average number of months spent in
each grade by Army enlisted men in general (as
of 1964).

The imputed value of medical services (at an
annual rate of $253) was added to each of these
sums to obtain average military earnings which can
be anticipated by a young man who enlists in the
Army for a three-year period during the specified
calendar quarter.

W_{m2} The average military earnings which can be anticipated by a young man enlisting in the armed
forces for his first term were calculated by
essentially the same process described under
W_{m1} above. However, the results were weighted
by the number of first enlistments into the
different services.

U_1 Monthly figures on the number of unemployed
males aged 16-19 and the number of males aged
16-19 in the civilian labor force were obtained from the Bureau of Labor Statistics.
These figures were added in three-month clusters
to obtain the number of unemployed and the number in the labor force during each quarter from
1958 to 1969.

The number in the labor force during each quarter was then divided into the number unemployed during the same quarter to obtain quarterly unemployment rates.

U_2 Quarterly unemployment rates for males aged 16-21 whose "major activity" was other than attending school were obtained by the process described under U_1 above. However, the series for U_2 does not begin until 1961; unemployment data on this group were not gathered by the Bureau of Labor Statistics prior to that time.

U_3 Quarterly unemployment rates for males aged 18-19 were obtained by the process described under U_1 above. However, rates were not calculated for any quarter after 1965.

A_1 For the period beginning with the third quarter of 1958 and ending with the third quarter of 1963, the number of accessions to the Army per quarter (in all mental categories) was drawn from annual reports of the qualitative distribution of military manpower program.

Beginning with the fourth quarter of 1963, when monthly reports of qualitative distribution became available, the numbers of accessions to the Army per month were added in three-month clusters to obtain the total number of accessions to the Army in a specified calendar quarter.

A_2 For the period beginning with the third quarter of 1958 and ending with the third quarter of 1963, the number of accessions to all services per quarter (in all mental categories) was obtained by adding the number of accessions to each of the services per quarter.

Beginning with the fourth quarter of 1963, when monthly reports of qualitative distribution became available, the numbers of accessions to the Department of Defense per month were added in three-month clusters to obtain the total number of accessions to all services per quarter.

199

DATA FOR REGRESSION ANALYSIS OF TIME-SERIES ON ENLISTMENTS

Calendar Year	Quarter	E_1	E_2	P_1	P_2	W_c	W_{m1}	W_{m2}	U_1	U_2	U_3	A_1	A_2
1958	3	28,311	81,679	1,791,827	4,088,225	$7,078	$7,431	$6,933	.162	000	.173	66,933	126,038
1958	4	21,638	54,978	1,779,682	4,175,962	7,082	7,431	6,933	.154	000	.157	51,236	97,814
1959	1	23,838	63,575	1,786,636	4,284,386	7,086	7,431	6,933	.169	000	.170	51,454	94,814
1959	2	20,653	54,573	1,853,276	4,424,659	7,090	7,431	6,933	.159	000	.145	37,027	73,383
1959	3	26,062	80,894	1,923,220	4,554,852	7,095	7,431	6,933	.142	000	.138	52,290	111,118
1959	4	20,402	58,954	1,948,532	4,641,245	7,228	7,431	6,933	.148	000	.146	46,255	88,013
1960	1	24,877	69,643	1,946,154	4,715,569	7,361	7,431	6,933	.161	000	.162	40,125	91,481
1960	2	23,098	67,809	1,962,457	4,806,578	7,494	7,431	6,933	.169	000	.150	46,270	98,877
1960	3	29,535	97,508	1,993,768	4,888,447	7,628	7,431	6,933	.135	000	.135	52,644	131,570
1960	4	23,017	63,849	1,989,942	4,945,496	7,622	7,431	6,933	.139	000	.159	47,854	95,381
1961	1	30,442	76,320	1,965,450	5,005,851	7,615	7,431	6,933	.196	.204	.203	42,074	93,641
1961	2	24,311	67,624	1,986,529	5,091,233	7,609	7,431	6,933	.191	.170	.176	25,407	74,158
1961	3	34,689	109,596	2,044,679	5,233,381	7,602	7,431	6,933	.148	.133	.136	81,417	161,864
1961	4	28,403	76,754	2,022,267	5,339,542	7,707	7,431	6,933	.156	.139	.146	87,946	141,842
1962	1	31,689	84,145	1,898,677	5,327,937	7,813	7,431	6,933	.171	.179	.170	64,889	124,851
1962	2	22,438	66,643	1,853,987	5,400,562	7,918	7,431	6,933	.165	.140	.139	41,779	90,132
1962	3	29,633	91,785	1,910,547	5,544,717	8,024	7,431	6,933	.122	.114	.119	47,441	113,930
1962	4	21,389	58,449	1,944,711	5,652,952	8,050	7,431	6,933	.137	.118	.131	37,149	76,662
1963	1	24,625	69,318	1,975,122	5,715,252	8,076	7,571	7,074	.185	.174	.178	43,745	91,474
1963	2	20,162	59,568	1,862,641	5,772,332	8,102	7,571	7,074	.205	.142	.178	45,536	88,303
1963	3	28,030	91,418	1,682,882	5,872,212	8,127	7,571	7,074	.150	.131	.140	59,471	130,626
1963	4	20,720	61,267	1,556,677	6,053,096	8,192	8,021	7,276	.153	.128	.144	71,129	115,340

Calendar Year	Quarter	E_1	E_2	P_1	P_2	W_c	W_{m1}	W_{m2}	U_1	U_2	U_3	A_1	A_2
1964	1	29,438	77,628	1,461,587	6,510,434	$8,257	$8,021	$7,276	.176	.168	.160	77,903	129,571
1964	2	22,347	65,318	1,454,550	7,088,955	8,322	8,021	7,276	.192	.135	.161	50,994	95,810
1964	3	28,833	90,145	1,506,077	7,458,126	8,388	8,021	7,276	.131	.114	.133	48,056	112,857
1964	4	18,640	51,334	1,564,692	7,707,322	8,760	8,089	7,307	.139	.120	.135	41,898	78,682
1965	1	21,634	63,527	1,529,216	8,035,542	9,132	8,089	7,307	.156	.131	.140	40,686	89,570
1965	2	20,492	66,694	1,433,770	8,327,355	9,504	8,089	7,307	.172	.124	.157	69,077	120,315
1965	3	30,453	113,900	1,277,522	8,431,778	9,876	8,722	7,889	.121	.100	.106	95,728	187,980
1965	4	30,837	102,679	1,060,809	8,407,628	9,590	8,722	7,889	.119	.087	.099	136,269	219,976
1966	1	47,349	127,292	808,250	8,405,124	9,305	8,722	7,889	.125	.096	000	137,170	237,304
1966	2	29,839	135,026	624,098	8,424,862	9,020	8,722	7,889	.143	.103	000	119,906	232,494
1966	3	43,644	128,857	667,635	8,395,342	8,735	8,895	8,029	.099	.081	000	164,257	255,969
1966	4	38,444	88,371	712,792	8,368,106	8,861	8,895	8,029	.105	.083	000	147,492	207,310
1967	1	29,546	76,350	672,189	8,484,132	8,987	8,895	8,029	.125	.100	000	83,076	138,889
1967	2	27,996	79,715	739,398	8,696,199	9,113	8,895	8,029	.129	.116	000	86,931	149,362
1967	3	39,739	104,853	842,644	8,791,905	9,240	9,376	8,463	.111	.091	000	128,990	207,632
1967	4	30,400	83,490	872,238	8,873,797	9,321	9,376	8,463	.131	.091	000	100,787	165,880
1968	1	39,300	98,628	830,716	9,027,381	9,402	9,376	8,463	.130	.109	000	149,397	222,267
1968	2	39,269	99,637	756,875	9,070,654	9,483	9,376	8,463	.120	.108	000	155,260	235,349
1968	3	42,298	114,486	752,777	9,009,846	9,563	9,840	8,822	.103	.086	000	105,722	193,596
1968	4	29,305	94,760	837,812	9,058,960	9,644	9,840	8,822	.114	.086	000	77,533	161,664
1969	1	32,161	95,589	868,629	9,208,421		9,840	8,822		.102	000	137,197	220,767

SOURCES OF RAW DATA FOR REGRESSION ANALYSIS
OF TIME SERIES ON ENLISTMENTS

E_1, E_2 Annual Report of the Qualitative Distribution of Military Manpower Program. DD-MP &
A_1, A_2 R (M)-344. Prepared by Executive Agent,
Office of the Adjutant General, Department
of the Army. Fiscal years 1959-61.

Annual Report of the Qualitative Distribution of Military Manpower Program. DD-MP &
R (M)-344. Prepared by Office of Personnel
Operations, Department of the Army. Fiscal
year 1962.

Twelfth Annual Report; Qualitative Distribution of Military Manpower Program. DD-MP &
R (M)-344. Prepared by Procurement Division,
Office of the Deputy Chief of Staff for Personnel, Headquarters, United States Continental Army Command. Fiscal year 1963.

Thirteenth Annual Report; Qualitative Distribution of Military Manpower Program.
DD-MP & R (M)-344. Headquarters, United
States Army Recruiting Command. Fiscal
year 1964.

Personnel Procurement: Qualitative Distri-
bution of Military Accessions and Rejections.
USCONARC Pamphlet No. 601 (13-23). DD-MP &
R (M)-344. Headquarters, United States
Continental Army Command, Fort Monroe,
Virginia. October, 1963-August, 1964.

Personnel Procurement: Qualitative Distri-
bution of Military Accessions and Rejections.
USAREC Pamphlet No. 601 (1-10). DD-MP & R
(M)-344. Headquarters, United States Army
Recruiting Command, Fort Monroe, Virginia.
September, 1964-June, 1965.

Qualitative Distribution of Military Accessions and Rejections. DD-M (M) 663. Headquarters, United States Army Recruiting

202

Command, Fort Monroe, Virginia. July, 1965–
May, 1966.

*Armed Forces Examining and Entrance Station
Qualitative Distribution of Male Enlistments,
Inductions and Rejections*. DD-M (M) 663.
Headquarters, United States Army Recruiting
Command, Hampton, Virginia. June, 1966–
April, 1969.

P_1, P_2 Monthly report on number and percent of
classified registrants. Research and Statistics Division, National Headquarters,
Selective Service System. July, 1958–March,
1969. Drawn from Selective Service System
Form 116.

*Annual Report of the Director of Selective
Service*. Washington: U.S. Government
Printing Office, fiscal years 1956–67.

*Semi-Annual Report of the Director of
Selective Service*. Washington: U.S.
Government Printing Office, fiscal year
1968.

W_c *Current Population Reports; Consumer Income*.
Series P-60, Nos. 33, 35, 37, 39, 41, 43,
47, 51, 53, 60. U.S. Bureau of the Census,
Department of Commerce. Washington: U.S.
Government Printing Office, 1958–67.

W_{m1}, W_{m2} Unpublished study prepared by Joseph Glenn
for a Department of Defense pay study group,
1962.

U_1, U_2,   Unpublished statistics of the U.S. Bureau
U_3 of Labor Statistics, Department of Labor,
1958–69.

DATA FOR CROSS-SECTION ANALYSIS OF ENLISTMENTS

Region	Enlistment Rates (Mental Categories I-III) 1963[a]		Estimated No-Draft Enlistment Rates (Mental Categories I-III) 1963[b]		Civilian Earnings 1964[c]	Military Earnings 1964[d]	1 Minus Unemployment Rate[e]
	DOD	Army	DOD	Army			
New England	.2288	.0676	.1255	.0336	$3,567	$2,577	.887
Middle Atlantic	.1947	.0564	.1133	.0297	3,748	2,577	.858
South Atlantic	.1947	.0697	.1435	.0465	2,849	2,577	.906
South	.2120	.0800	.1442	.0493	2,441	2,577	.861
Western South	.1950	.0646	.1417	.0425	3,148	2,577	.908
Great Lakes	.1803	.0611	.1008	.0310	4,184	2,577	.889
Great Plains	.1735	.0523	.0750	.0205	3,725	2,577	.940
Mountain	.2009	.0640	.1127	.0325	3,640	2,577	.902
Pacific	.2134	.0711	.1111	.0335	4,257	2,577	.838

[a] 1963 enlistees per 10,000 of the physically and mentally qualified 17-20-year-old male full-time labor force.

[b] Estimated 1963 no-draft-motivated enlistments per 10,000 of the physically and mentally qualified 17-20-year-old male full-time labor force.

[c] Mean income of full-time civilian nonveterans aged 16-21 not in school.

[d] Average over first four years of service.

[e] Unemployment rates of civilian nonveterans aged 16-21, not enrolled in school, as of October, 1964.

Source: Stuart H. Altman, "Earnings, Unemployment, and the Supply of Enlisted Volunteers," The Journal of Human Resources (1969), Vol. 4, No. 1, 38-59.

SELECTED BIBLIOGRAPHY

SELECTED BIBLIOGRAPHY

Abelson, Philip M. "Student Anxiety," _Science_, CLVIII (December 1, 1967), 1139.

Altman, Stuart H. "Earnings, Unemployment, and the Supply of Enlisted Volunteers," _The Journal of Human Resources_ (1969), Vol. 4, No. 1, pp. 38-59.

Altman, Stuart H., and Alan E. Fechter. "The Supply of Military Personnel in the Absence of a Draft," _American Economic Review_, LVII, 2 (May, 1967), 19-31.

Clague, Ewan. _Unemployment--Past, Present, and Future._ American Enterprise Institute for Public Policy Research, Analysis No. 12. June 27, 1969.

"Cost/Effectiveness of Reenlistment Incentives," _Appendix to Annex G, Navy Manpower Considerations, 1970-1980_, Study 13, Institute of Naval Studies. February, 1966.

Fisher, Anthony C. "The Cost of the Draft and the Cost of Ending the Draft," _American Economic Review_, Vol. LIX, No. 3. June, 1969.

The Image of the Army: Army Veterans, General Public, High School Educators, and Vietnam Army Veterans in College Appraise the U.S. Army. Prepared for N. W. Ayer and Sons, Inc., and the U.S. Army. Princeton, N.J.: Opinion Research Corporation, August, 1969.

Kim, K. H. "An Econometric Growth Model of the U.S., 1902-52, With Emphasis on Monetary Controls." 1963. (Unpublished paper.)

Kim, K. H., *et al*. *An Army 75 Personnel Procurement Concept*. Battelle Memorial Institute, July 31, 1968. For the Department of the Army, Contract DAHC 19 67 C 0031.

Oi, Walter Y. "The Economic Cost of the Draft-- Discussion," *American Economic Review*, LVII, 2 (May, 1967), 39-70.

Reference Materials from the Department of Defense Study of the Draft. Office of Secretary of Defense for Manpower, July, 1966.

Solow, Robert M. "Investment and Technical Progress," *Mathematical Methods in the Social Sciences: Proceedings of the First Stanford Symposium*, Stanford Mathematical Studies in the Social Sciences, IV. Stanford: Stanford University Press, 1960, Vol. 39, No. 3, pp. 89-104.

Solow, Robert M. "Technical Change and the Aggregate Production Function," *Review of Economics and Statistics* (1957), Vol. 39, No. 3, 312-20.

ABOUT THE AUTHORS

K. H. KIM, currently director of research at Jack Faucett Associates, Inc., in Washington, D.C., has specialized in economics and operations research. For several years, he served as consultant to the Department of Defense in manpower planning and force development. At the time of this study, he was director of the economics department of Leo Kramer, Inc. Mr. Kim was formerly a senior economist at Battelle Memorial Institute and vice-president of the Nam-Sun Manufacturing Company. He was educated at the University of Pennsylvania and at Stanford University, where he was a University Fellow at the Institute for Mathematical Studies in the Social Sciences.

SUSAN FARRELL is a member of the economics research staff of Leo Kramer, Inc. She served for three years as speechwriter and as legislative assistant in the areas of social security, pension systems, and welfare programs to a member of the U.S. House of Representatives. Miss Farrell has also been a researcher and analyst in public health at the Legislative Reference Service of the Library of Congress. She was educated at the University of Michigan.

EWAN CLAGUE was Commissioner of the U.S. Bureau of Labor Statistics from 1946 to 1965. He is currently a senior associate of Leo Kramer, Inc. When the Social Security Act was passed, Dr. Clague became director of the Board's Bureau of Research and Statistics. Later, he served as administrator of the federal unemployment insurance program. Dr. Clague was educated at the University of Washington and the University of Wisconsin. His book on the Bureau of Labor Statistics has been published in Praeger's series on federal departments and agencies.